Crap CVs

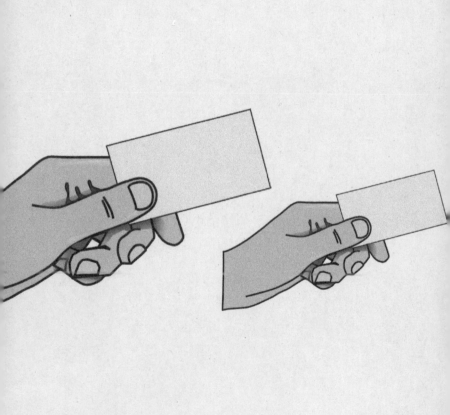

Crap CVs

Jenny
Crompton

PENGUIN BOOKS

PENGUIN BOOKS

Published by the Penguin Group
Penguin Books Ltd, 80 Strand, London WC2R ORL, England
Penguin Group (USA) Inc., 375 Hudson Street, New York, New York 10014, USA
Penguin Group (Canada), 90 Eglinton Avenue East, Suite 700, Toronto, Ontario, Canada M4P 2Y3
(a division of Pearson Penguin Canada Inc.)
Penguin Ireland, 25 St Stephen's Green, Dublin 2, Ireland (a division of Penguin Books Ltd)
Penguin Group (Australia), 707 Collins Street, Melbourne, Victoria 3008,
Australia (a division of Pearson Australia Group Pty Ltd)
Penguin Books India Pvt Ltd, 11 Community Centre,
Panchsheel Park, New Delhi – 110 017, India
Penguin Group (NZ), 67 Apollo Drive, Rosedale, Auckland 0632, New Zealand
(a division of Pearson New Zealand Ltd)
Penguin Books (South Africa) (Pty) Ltd, Block D, Rosebank Office Park, 181 Jan Smuts Avenue,
Parktown North, Gauteng 2193, South Africa

Penguin Books Ltd, Registered Offices: 80 Strand, London WC2R ORL, England

www.penguin.com

First published 2014

014

Text design by Claire Mason
Typeset by Penguin Books
Printed in Great Britain by Clays Ltd, Elcograf S.p.A.

ISBN: 978-1-405-91867-1

www.greenpenguin.co.uk

To all the hopelessly unemployed

CONTENTS

DEAR SIR OR MADMAN . . .

Crap Covering Letters

To concern whom it may concern . . .

Hello. Please find my resume.

To Home-Ever it Concerns . . .

Dear Sir/Modem . . .

Dear Sir or Madman . . .

Welcome To . . .
My!
Most!
Awesome!
RESUME!!
AWWWWWWWW YEAHHHHHHH!

I am foreign so sorry for any incontinence.

Can u tell me more about this position?

Hi there,

You're probably reading a lot of applications. And you're probably not enjoying yourself. I'm writing this cover letter, and I'm not enjoying myself either. So, let me cut to the chase.

I won't pretend that your company's mission is my passion, but I do think sales are quite interesting. If you hire me, I'll show up for the hours you expect me to 99 per cent of the time – which, let's face it, already puts me ahead of most other applicants.

I was well liked at college, and you know the importance of that for sales. I'm willing to bet you won't like the personality of most of the people who appear to be 'qualified' for this entry-level position, based on the fact that if they've had time to meet the qualifications for this job by the time they graduated college, they likely have no social skills. As someone who was voted 'Life of the Party' both in high school and in my fraternity, you won't have to worry about hiring some stiff loser who will poorly represent the youthful image of your company, or any other worries you might have about your new hire being a cultural fit.

You'll notice that I haven't talked about what skills I have yet. Do I honestly need to? I went to an elite institution and we all know I'll figure out how to use whatever programs you'd like me to toil away on. Working at your company isn't rocket science.

Get back to me if you're looking for someone you'll actually enjoy working with.

Please check my profile (enclosed herewith) for more details, although I've presented a crux herewith in this introductory note.

This is my CV I am intrested in any job opening use have avaiable if u could please send a vercation that you reciceved the email.

I am superior to anyone else you could hire.

I be no stranger to double-entry. I loves numbers, and my wife and I loves journals and ledgers! Can also do tricky sums when I puts my mind to it. Computor litrate.

✓

You will want me to be Head Honcho in no time.

To Whom It May Concern,

I am writing this cover letter not because I am desperate to work for an esteemed corporation such as yours, but because I'm just desperate. Period. For the sake of my sanity, please hire me. I'm sure I must have at least one redeeming quality that makes me slightly qualified for this position. Thank you for your consideration – or for at least pretending to review my CV.

＊ Enclosed please find my resume. You mention in your ad that you require a writing sample, but I send out at least fifty resumes a week, and writing samples are expensive.

I am sure you have looked through several resumes and cover letters with the same information about work experience, education and references . . . I am not going to give you any of that stuff.

✓

Re: summer internship

Good day.
My name is Pablo Mustafa. I am a former painting assistant to Jesus Christ and Takashi Murakami. I am twenty-three years old and as such would love to work for a summer sweeping floors and filing, despite my college education at Oxford and my noble upbringing. Furthermore I would further deprave myself and my skills by working for free. Thank you and I look forward to our interview.

Please note from my CV I have six years' buying, negotiating and sock-control experience.

I am a bit dyslexic so apologies for the scatological nature of my covering letter.

✓

To Whom It May Concern,
Resume is something for appeal myself, Let's have a appeal time!

My big reason of come to Canada, Europe, North and South America travel.

So I apply to your shop! I am not a good English user. But when I was in korea, everybody call me 'Ace, you are a best!' at Factory, hotel, farm, restaurant, mart.

Especially, I love always smile working environment, too short time I worked custom service but It is best work in my life and I want to feel again.

By the way, I worked server and kitchen help in Canada. I am always good when I am working, please feel me.

I have brave fight to wild bear.

I have strong arm lift to wild bear.

I am so fast more than train.

I can work without pay right now! I do not care when you will pay me. Please pay me after you think I have Qualification for get a pay.

Why do I love accounting: My passion for accounting started since I was a child. Not because I knew at the time what accounting was, but I loved working with numbers. From the first days at the school my uncle told me that 'X' is a wild beast, and I have to chase it. After catching it gave me lots of pleasure. Apparently that was the start of my interest and passion for numbers, which later on became accounting.

I kick ass. See resume for proof.

I am no good at my job and get bored very easily so I'm looking for something different and was wondering if you have any opportunities that may be of interest to me?

I am a dilettante and a factotum whose knowledge of English and its usage mark me as an ideal candidate.

As a finance major I am extremely interested in capital markets, assessments of project risk and budgets, but above all things technical, I simply want to make a difference – to 'leave my mark'. The following list best describes the type of person I am and want to become.

The following goals must be accomplished and WILL be accomplished

Goals are listed in order of importance

1. Get married
2. Never divorce
3. Go to church regularly
4. Never become idle in my self-education
5. Raise Christian children who are better people than myself
6. Become well respected in my profession
7. Enjoy going to work

✱ Hi am attaching CV please look at it
and get back to me ASAP.

Please check out my CV and then sign me up for whatever work you have available.

I noticed a typo on your website and I can tell you that would NOT happen if I worked for you. I'll tell you what it is if you invite me in for an interview.

I'm intrested to here more about that. I'm working today in a furniture factory as a drawer.

Time is very valuable and it should be always used to achieve optimum results and I believe it should not be played around with.

I believe that weakness is the first level of strength, given the right attitude and driving force.

I am attaching a letter of recommendation from my mother.

I hope you don't take this the wrong way, but as an example of my 'no pain no gain' attitude I am attaching several photographs my ex took of me doing one-armed push-ups (sorry I was naked but you can't really see it!).

I am fully aware of the king of attention this position requires.

I'm a guy with an enviable history. Some would say a rogue, I would say at least a lovable rogue. Just like my mentor Jon Bon Jovi, I've seen a million faces and I've rocked them all.

I➡✗ ✗ ➡✗ ❄☐◆❈❇✳❀▲◆▼➡☐✗ ➡✚I❄☀

I've spent a considerable time both high above and deep below ground. I like the perspective from both places. It's a shame so many people never look beyond the front of their noses. I like to see the angles others miss. I've listened to a million stories, and told a few of my own. I'd like to hear your story, because there's nothing like a good story. Except perhaps Dutch liquorice.

Please don't take this the wrong way, I have every respect for you as a person but it does aggreive me when people don't realize how employable I actually am, although self-praise is no reccomendation.

 Strange as it may seem, but I've noticed that what I am doing today, others will do a couple of years later.

Instead of being a follower I prefer to be a leader. I never fail to do what I believe is right and I don't care what other people think about me. Not a good sign but again, I see 'being successful' as making it despite great adversity, rather than making it by using other people's weaknesses. No wonder I have no money.

Although making lots of money is commonly used as a measure of success, profitability is not something that interests me.

▶ Although I have a can-do attitude, i.e., I'd rather have a go at something than just talk about it, I am also very easily bored, so I prefer a chaotic environment.

Please consider me for shit job.

I live my life by the standards of the three P's: Professionalism, Personality, Perseverance. Also Precognition, but that's more of a skill than a standard. I predict any position I take, I will thrive and grow, and if properly nurtured and cajoled, I will rise to the utmost levels of your expectations. You might consider me a silver-winged unicorn soaring over (and outshining) the brightest and most colourful of rainbows as angelic voices sing a heavenly and over-modulated version of 'Come Down'.

Thing is, I won't become this single-horned soaring beauty if not given the opportunity to speak words in between songs twice every thirty minutes. That ninety-eight seconds of verbiage per hour (about five minutes total per four-hour shift) is a dream within a dream with an afterthought wrapped up in a memory and intertwined with the desires of my soul.

Let me know when you would like to have me spread my voice of warm golden butter across your airwaves and straight to the thighs, hips and buttocks of your listeners' ears.

✓

I appreciate your time and mine. I look forward to meeting and impressing you.

✓

I hope to have some facial conversation with you at your convenience, so that I can furnish you with detailed information about myself.

✓

Just as an aside, as well as an actual job, I am also seeking wealthy investors in my freelance tech startup.

Dear Human Resources Manager,

I am applying for the job I saw posted today on your Place of Business website. This ad caught my attention because it is a job posting and I need a job. Already you can see we're going to make a perfect match.

Your need of someone to work in your Place of Business is a terrific fit with my background in working. Why would I want to work for your Place of Business? I like food. I enjoy having money to buy food, and a place to live. I've also got other bills. You need an employee; I'm great at being an employee! I'm even better at getting paid. You need someone to work, and I need to work. It's win-win. I don't think there could be a better fit in this world than you needing someone to work and my needing someplace to work. As you can see, I'm a very motivated person who will enjoy working.

You can email me or call me anytime, day or night, because I'm currently *not* working. So how 'bout it?

The engineering of your company website looks lazy and ineffective. The colour scheme is disconcerting to my eyes.

i am writting to aPPly to be the new DireCtor of the
NatioNaL RailwAy MuseuM. i am only 6 but i think i
can do tHis Job.

i have an eLectricaL train trAck. i am Good on my train
track, i caN control 2 trains At oncE.

HopeFully i can come anD Meet you foR an inTervieW.

I guess the only reason I'm applying is
because I studied journalism. I don't read
much of the magazine you mention in your
job requirement but I do have an analytical
mind. I know I am not tailor-made for the
job and I am only available for the next
three months in any case – nevertheless,
this looked interesting. It was fun applying!

Attached, please find my resume. I would LOVE to be
a lifestyle/Wall Street intern as both topics fascinate
me and I have great experience in both. The only
caveat is I have to do this during
non-working hours. Please let me know if
you have any questions.

I'll cut to the chase. It's definitely time for a career change!

What I'm capable of: following house style, typing 65 wpm, proofing, trafficking (publishing, not narcotics – would I be trolling the web for jobs if that were the case?), Quark, Adobe, Outlook and MS Office (only average at Excel).

What I'm not capable of: HTML.

I'm sick of writing these pedestrian cover letters and you're sick of reading them. I won't gush with some sanctimonious speech about your company. I only apply to companies for whom I'm interested in working.

I do not have any relevant work experience but I have always been an avid reader and had my own blog a couple of years ago. I received some feedback from the grand-father of a friend of mine, and it was very positive. I did not continue writing it but I have always felt 'the pull of the pen'.

✳ I'm a writer and artist who recently relocated to New York to actually work in one of my fields, only to put a lot of time into cover letters that never get acknowledged. This really surprises me. Since I moved here solely for career purposes and don't really have any friends yet, I'm in a perfect position to make work my life.

I really don't think you will find a better candidate for this job. I also feel confident that there are lots of improvements I could make to your company.

I was excited to find your posting in search of a Features Editor. In every regard, my qualifications appear to be consistent with your desires, and from my critical evaluation of your newsroom and its inhabitants, I really think that it is meant to be. I hope this, the fifteen billionth letter you've received today, convinces you of my dedication and limitless energy – enough so that you feel you must meet me immediately.

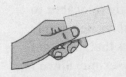

Writing has always inspired me, an exhilarating rollercoaster of a ride, traversing my mind to places and feelings refreshingly cathartic. The ability to delve deep into one's Pandora box, pulling out a rabbit of unbridled emotions and brilliance, is tantamount to my writing. It is this confidence in my abilities, combined with an insatiable drive to succeed, that ignites this author's race car.

I was pleased to discover, through my clandestine Alaskan network, that you have not yet finalized a new law clerk for the upcoming year. I hope you find this letter portentously post facto rather than unskillfully delinquent. I wish to spare you the unleavened hardtrack of your sensible, standard cover letter and instead appeal to your irrational masculine avatar through a reflective vignette. Alaska will play setting to my further evolution. Let me know if you've got anything.

Dear Sir or Madame,

I am an ambitious undergraduate at NYU triple majoring in Mathematics, Economics, and Computer Science. I am a punctual, personable and shrewd individual, yet I have a quality that I pride myself on more than any of these.

I am unequivocally the most unflaggingly hard worker I know, and I love self-improvement. I have always felt that my time should be spent wisely, so I continuously challenge myself; I left my previous university because the work was too easy. Once I realized I could achieve a perfect grade point average while holding a part-time job at NYU, I decided to redouble my effort by taking two honors classes and holding two part-time jobs. That semester I achieved a 3.93, and in the same time I managed to bench double my bodyweight and do thirty-five pull-ups.

I say these things only because solid evidence is more convincing than unverifiable statements, and I want to demonstrate that I am a hard worker. I know that the employees in your firm will push me to excellence; in fact, one of the reasons I chose investment banking over any other division was that I know it is difficult.

I am proficient in several programming languages, and I can pick up a new one very quickly. For instance, I learned a year's worth in twenty-seven days on my own. I am proficient with Bloomberg terminals, excellent with Excel, and can perform basic office functions with terrifying efficiency. My most recent employer found me so useful that he promoted me to a role usually reserved for Masters students, but he gave the title to me so that he could give me more work.

Please realize that I am not a braggart or conceited, I just want to outline my usefulness. Egos can be a huge liability, and I try not to have one.

I see from your Facebook profile pictures that you visited Nepal in April 2008 – I stayed at that same hotel on my way to teach blind nuns English!

*   hello im qualified english teacher with particulier interest in creative writting.

Making me an addition to this workforce will not be a problem.

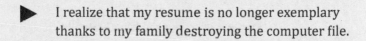

> ► I realize that my resume is no longer exemplary thanks to my family destroying the computer file.

I am very interested in the account stuff position.

Important note: Resume adjectives and job descriptions have not been altered despite labour market conditions. I have not embellished my resume nor changed it, except to incorporate additional details and in some instances to delete wordiness.

Even if I don't get the job, it's OK. It's worth putting in the time and effort writing this resume.

Does your printed material scream 'LOOK OVER HEAR'? If not, why pay the high price for something that doesn't catch the reader's attention.

I am eager to put my MacGyver-like design ability to use in the workplace. I'm sure you receive hundreds of these letters a week, but how many of those people have built an entire campaign with nothing more than old barbed wire and used Popsicle sticks? None? I've never done that either, but it would be a neat trick. I would like to come by and show you my work in the hope of making something of my life so I can move out of my parents' basement.

'Twas four weeks after Christmas
And all throughout a certain company,
Human Relations pondered over
Who would be the next intern/employee?

The staff in their cubicles, all snug in their chairs,
While visions of lunch were their only main cares.
The big boss in his office, and me still at Miami,
Both nervous and wondering: our hands remained clammy.

When out in the mailroom there arose such a clatter,
Employees from all over crowded to see what was the matter.
Back in my apartment with a smile laid back,
I knew once they'd opened my letter; there was no turning back.

As ivory goes along with a substance called soap,
Everyone looked at each other with a small gleam of hope.
'It's time to stop letting all the normal folk dance,
And open our eyes, and give this chick a chance!'

✓

I've posted my resume to this website, where you can create a profile to log in and then download it within the next three days.

✓

I'm even more computer illiterate than my resume shows.

✓

I have applied to over 200 positions within the last two years.

✓

I would appreciate the opportunity to review my qualifications.

Today is the first day of my life. Last year was a tremendous year for personal growth, insight and maturity. I courted that growth. This year I want to 'take the world by storm'. I am terrified of the all-out approach I sense in my spirit. However, I am not scared enough to let it stop me. I will go and push and strive until I have reached the finish line. I will sacrifice anything but my God (morals) and my family. Pride has no place in my new life. I will be striving for perfection.

I implore you, take this full-of-life, creative, fun, hardworking, quick learner, hands-on, intelligent, good-looking individually, and help him by giving him the best possible experience, so he can continue the legacy of provided high-level, knock-your-socks-off advertising.

Originally from Vietnam, I also offer expertise in the following areas:

★ Asian cuisine: I deliver, in-box or out-of-the-box
★ Traditional massage: I satisfy Client above their expectation
★ Karaoke singing: but also a lot of listening, listening and listening to Client

Would you like to taste any of those, please feel free to contact me.

Your website is very unfriendly and may sway some clients into not working with you. Your website thinks that it is witty, but comes off very dull and cheesy.

I do not seriously feel I am readily employable. While this statement does not fit well into potential employment situations, my belief is that complete disclosure is the only reasonable approach.

✳ Although I am seeking a nursing job, the fact that I have no actual medical experience may seem discouraging.

✓

Hire me, I have great hair.

✓

I am applying for this position to offer the perfect environment to demonstrate my many different talents.

**I don't usually toot my own horn,
but in this case I will go right ahead and do so.
TOOT TOOT!**

✓

I'm the best accountant you're ever going to find. If your company doesn't want to pay for the high quality, don't bother calling.

This is the first time in my long and impressive career I've had to actually seek work.

HI,
  MY NAME IS EUGENE.
  I'M FROM UKRAINE, AND WERY INTERESTING ABOUT ADVERTISMENT ...
  I HAVE SOME INTERESTING AND ABSOLUTELY NEW IDEAS (for example about car brands) ... BUT IN OUR FUKING (sorry) COUNTRY ITS UNREAL TO DO OWN BUSSINESS ... MAY BE YOU WANT TO WORK WITH US? ITS WILL BE REALLY GOOD ...
  BEST REGARDS!
  eugene

▌➡𝗫 𝗫 ➫𝗫 ❋▢◗◆❋❋❋❋✿▲◆▼➡▢𝗫 ➡➕▌❋☀

I need real-world experience and after reviewing your website I get the impressing that your company believes in maintain a lax work environment while efficiently meeting the needs of it's customers (right?).

I've given a year of my life in a minimum-security work camp and I'm nearing work release status. I need to connect with open-minded people like myself! My crime was a 'non-violent, victimless' one. I'm hoping this letter is reaching people who have or do smoke weed.

I would like to do first project for you without any payment or salary. Just to prove my creativity. This is to win your confidence to give me a Just to prove that I can add wing to your agency to fly and reach the height of success. Though it may sound big but I believe in myself and have enough confident to win your trust on me by my work. This will give both of us to understand better.

That I offer my services at all, you may take as a complement, since I am one of the new wave of workers more interested in the quality of my work than the new-fangaled fast-buck concepts of the past few years.

Hello. This is my second email to you regarding the question that I had about the internship position at your company. I find it very unprofessional that you have gone an entire day without responding to me and it makes me question the type of office you work in and whether I even want to be an intern at your company. If you could please answer my question (I have attached yesterday's e-mail below in case you forgot) I would appreciate it and it will help me decide if I will apply for your internship position.

Please remember that I will be taking into consideration the lack of professionalism you have demonstrated by not answering my question in a prompt manner. I'm sorry you have gotten us off on the wrong foot. I hope that you can get your act together in the future.

I hope that we disposition participate in a reciprocated hyperlink exchange. Disillusion admit me certain and take an wonderful day!

I cannot express to you how excited I got as I came across your website.

Hi Susan I found out ur mobile number & wanted 2 check we're still on 4 interview 2moro 3pm. Can't wait 2 meet u! Cheers, Steve.

✓

Deer Sir or Madam,

I have wanted to join _____ to work as a _____ from an early age as you are a big prestigious employer that lots of people want to work for and you offer high salaries. I would also like to work in another country and you are a global company.

Regards,
Frank

What's up.

I'd like to start off saying that whatever you want . . . I have.

The odds of me even getting a response is hilarious.

I have accumulated four years' experience as a receptionist in boring-ass office jobs. I have worked in customer service accumulative of four years as well. It was in retail and sucked because I would rather sit than stand for eight hours at Urban Outfitters on the promenade. Arranging shoes at 2 a.m. in women's sales is basically slavery.

I am also a stand-up comedian. It's debatable whether or not I am even funny.

I'm attractive and will not send in my picture because I stopped doing that at age twelve in AOL chat rooms.

Resume furnished upon request.

I know this is unpaid, but as a personal non-negotiable, money is a requirement.

Eagerly wanting income and a really cool fucking job,

Kathy

**Let's meet so you can 'ooh' and 'aah'
over my experience.**

This little pony graduated with highest honors. While at university he cultivated an ongoing love for . . .
COMPUTER SCIENCE AND MATHEMATICS!

For two years he worked as a tutor for the Computer Science department. He loves passing on his knowledge and getting everypony excited about computer science!

After graduation he galloped off to become a radio DJ and freelance web developer. He produces stunning, high-quality websites for all the nice ponies.

For a few months he dabbled in domestication, ensuring that thousands of hardworking ponies got quality catered lunches of grains, oats and grasses every day! The daily plough just wasn't for him, though, so he threw off the bit and bridle and galloped away.

The adventure is far from over . . . What will this little pony do next? Who knows??

GET READY TO GET BLOWN AWAY BY RICKY SANTANGELO.

RICKY'S STORY

RICKY's seen it all. Everything from being born in the middle of a tornado and given a 75 per cent chance of living to running with the biggest rock stars of the Eighties. RICKY SANTANGELO knows how to go big. But why not let RICKY tell the story himself.

Hey guys, RICKY SANTANGELO here. I've done some crazy shit, man. It has forged me into the man I am today. U need a dude that got what it takes, so let's make it happen WOO WOO. U need experience? Six years tour manager . . . three years security . . . four years guitar tech *WHITEFUCKINGSNAKE* followed by two years in jail, but then followed again by three more years as personal helper to David Coverdale. I made it big with music and now I'm ready for movies . . .

IF U TAKE ON RICKY as a client U WILL GET PAID.

Need more proof? Here's a quote from RICKY to

Jake: 'I'm gonna FUCKING DESTROY THE MOVIE WORLD.' And then Jake said back: 'MOVE OVER TOM CRUISE, TIME FOR THE NEW FUCKING BLOOD.'

If u don't call up RICKY SANTANGELO now someone else will and ur boss will fucking FIRE U FOR FUCKING UP.

PS I DON'T GOT A PHONE RIGHT NOW SO EMAIL ME.

I'm submitting my CV to spite my lack of HTML experience.

✗ ✗ ☞✗ ❄◻◗◆❄✳❅❆ ▲◆▼➥◻✗ ➥✚▮✺❂

RE: OFFICE MANAGER AT SOFTWARE COMPANY

This job is exactly the position I have been looking for! Forget all the other candidates. I am the BEST.

Organizing shit? Check.

Calling customers and shit? Double-check.

Customer support and shit? Mega-check.

Faxing numbers and shit? MOTHER-FLIPPING-CHECK ALL OVER THAT.

Don't believe me? Check this shit out:

I am devilishly handsome. I was prom king two years in a row with two different queens.

I am ridiculously smart. I can solve any Rubik's Cube in front of your face with my magic fingers. I will bring one to prove it.

I am good for office morale. When someone cries I am all sympathetic and shit.

Need my resume? Nope. Not when you got my FACTS!

I am honourable. I am the son of a librarian and a Capricorn.

I am brave. I fight crime at weekends. I don't wear a cape yo, that shit is for PIMPS.

I am dependable. Just call my name and I'll be there.

I'll pop in tomorrow to get my paperwork all signed up around 11 a.m. No need for an interview, trust me you will love me. I got your address from Google, because my internet research skills are the shit.

Love,
Ronald

PS My favourite colour is taupe because it rhymes with DOPE!

Thank you for taking the time to beet me for an interview.

Please hire me. I am the perfect candidate for this position. I am a champion, I never fail and plus I KNOW AND CAN DO ANYTHING AND EVERYTHING. Do you know aliens from outer space? NO!!! I didn't think so because the definition of alien is foreign or undiscovered, but guess what?? I DO KNOW ALIENS FROM OUTER SPACE!

Good morning,

Attached is my resume, along with a few writing samples. If you have any questions, please feel free to fucking contact me at james@.com. And if you don't I'm gonna be fucking pissed! So come on, stop bullshitting and call me ;)

Thanks Cunt!

Skateboarder from 1980s to present time. Job duties include hanging out with friends, drinking, smoking, doing tricks such as ollying and variations of it, such as incorporating the flip of the board and its rotation. In addition, the art of grinding, which includes making contact with any portion of the skateboard against an object other than the street (pavement). Don't get grinding confused with that cheesy song: 'There ain't nothing wrong with a little bump and grind'. This is a different kind of grinding. I am not a pervert. I am a gentleman, a scholar and, of course, as I had already mentioned during our earlier encounter, a PROFESSIONAL GENIUS. I can answer any question on *Jeopardy*. That's a TV show hosted by Alex Trebek.

My other work experience includes playing punk rock

music. I can play ANY song on the guitar. I can harmonize, match pitch for pitch and downright tear apart anyone's ass musically, on vocals as well. Seriously, I am a musical master. Don't worry, I have recordings to prove it and yes, I play by ear. I have only played in ska or punk bands, which includes The Bob Sagets. I operate an indie record label, which was established in 1999, but my parents don't think that is technically a REAL job.

Lastly, in high school I sold a shit load of weed, coke, pills, mushroom, acid, hash, opium and pharmaceuticals.

PS Sorry I will need to take an extended
lunch break on alternate Thursdays (10.45
a.m.–1 p.m.) to get my highlights done.
I waited eighteen months to get on this
salon's client list!!!

Hi douche, they call me Mike.
I am a Flash developer with eight years' experience. If there was one word to describe me it would be 'da-bomb'. If you think you're good at Flash, news flash: you're fuckin' wrong. Cause I will rock your shit right outta your ass with my mad skillz. You want banners?

Fuck you, those bitches are already done. You want 'e-learning'? I'll make a new category called 'e-takin'youtoschoolSON'. You want a video player? I'll bone your wife, punch you in the heart, prepare a five-course meal of salmon and steak with a side of crisp buttered Parisian asparagus that have just a hint of nutmeg cause it's my fuckin' cooking trademark, take a massive life-altering mega-dump, then when all that's done I'll karate-powerbomb an email your way saying that shit was done two hours ago and to stop wasting my amazing-as-fucking-shit time.

Do I want this job? Yeah. Fuck yeah. I'm willing to go down for this shit, if you catch my obvious drift. I'm talking swallow the gravy. Times are tough.

So use your face and listen to me through your eyes. If you want a normal developer, I can take a single hair, put it in a pot of dirt and grow you a 5-foot-9-inch 235-pound awesome developer named Larry who likes to go by the name of Lars, has a dog, an ex-wife, four kids, a slight liquor problem, but hell, who doesn't love a good drink now and then! Certainly not me, I love lots of drinks, all the fuckin' time! So you can do that and be OK, or you can hire me, a demi-god that likes coke. Your choice.

Fuck you.

✓

I BELIVE THAT IF I WERE TO BE ACCEPTED AS AN EMPLOY WITH YOUR COMPANY THAT YOU WOULD NOT BE DISAPOINTED WITH MY WORK ETHICS. I DO MY BEST TO ENSURE I KEEP WELL ATENDENTS AN A STEDDY ROUTINE GOOD COMUNACASHOIN BETWEEN ME A MY COWORKERS IS OF HIGH IMPORTENTS TO ME. WITH JUST OVER A YEAR OF COOKING EXPERIYINCE I AM LOOKING TO INCREECE IT WITH YOUR COMPANY.

I WOULD APRESHIATE THE OPRATUNATY TO SPEEK WITH YOU ABOUT MY CREDENSHELS AT A MUTUALLY COMVENIENT TIME.

I EARGLY AWATE YOUR PROMP RESPONSE IN HOPES.

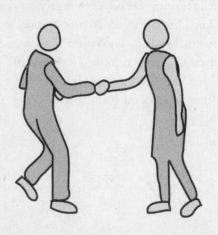

Within seeking employment, I chose to write your company in regards to becoming a part of your working environment. Heartfully, it would be the highest choice of my smile to discuss myself being hired for the above regarding or an opposite position that my work potential edifies. Please find enclosed an entailment of my work quality and references in making your decision to see the choice I am. To hear from you at your heart's delight would be the intrigue of my day.

✓

it's very simple mike. you are interested in my profile and i wanted to know how much you were able to pay. no response means: you either can't pay that much, or you only hire indians and pakistanis who don't ask for a good salary. but dude, i am neither indian or paki and i have never worked for less than 2000 usd/month.
You got it now!?

HERE ARE MY RESUME AND IM NOT SO INTEREST IN YOUR JOB THANKS MO

I also have some inventions for sale ! Some are certified , some are completed and the others are not certified or completed , only very good ideas . These ideas may have a very big value for who is concern or interristed in . Far from political effects , helping any human and any company at any country , for helping peace of the world . The new products may help me or anybody in the future !

New very simple device to measure the far distances
   approximately
A new shape of pencil
Very simple device to have electricity from air power
New shape for the keyboard
Improving fax machines
Paper not easy fired
Stopping the current of volcano faster
Electronic mirror
TV with some improvements
Methods very udeful for fidhing boats
Very fast printer
Easy storing files ((believe me))
Textile stronger for balloons, car wheel, fluids insulator
   (not rubber)

Hallo!! I have been very thrilled to find informations about your opening and I join hereto my CV. Apologies in advance: it is completely in French.

Dear Sir/Madam:

With this letter I would like to present and offer my services as profesional proofreader.

In certain moments of the editorial process, you could have some extra needs, and you could have to make use of the services of a freelance proofreader like me. I am prepared to offer so fluent, fast, serious work and good rates that our profesional relations will be good for the two of us.

For these reasons, I beg you to see attached CV, I hope you will find attractive and good to your needs. For further information, do not hesitate to contact to me. I will be willing to help you.

I have read everything I could find about you on the internet. You are a deeply fascinating person and I long to work for you.

Have a quick shufti at the attached doc
and let me know if you think it's worth me
applying. Don't want to waste your time
or mine!

I saw your job ad in the newspaper and my eyeballs literally popped out!

To whom it may concern,
I am currently incarcerated in the county jail where I was
ordered to participate in the work release programme
until I have brought my child support payments up to
date. Before I can enter the programme, however, I need
to find a job. I see you are currently looking for an
integration specialist, and as luck would have it I have
extensive experience integrating various systems. I am
the master!

Objective:
- To obtain a clerical position within your company.

Career highlights:
- Excellent customer service skills with an enjoyable phone voice
- Team player with independently abilities
- Knowledge of email, internet
- Type at an reasonable speed wit minot mistakes

*Every time I reread your detailed feedback on my interview I become more and more enlightened about myself and my various failings. Could you please add me to your database for future vacancies?

I'll be honest with you, Pauline, I am pretty much at the end of my job-seeking tether here.

Objective

A job in IT. After searching for a job for several months I'm not too particular any more. This can be a low rate of pay with the opportunity to advance as skills grow.

Work Experience

April 2003–current
Small contracts: maintaining software at a few small businesses. Earning a small income while looking for a regular job.

October 1998–April 2003
Programming: worked four and half years until a group of people from India came on-line and a bunch of us were laid off.

A Little History

My skill is to understand and find solutions to problems. My gift is plain intelligence, at the expense of understanding planning and value. I can do the innovative and apparently impossible in programming to solve a problem, the software being but a tool. The problem is that these innovative solutions may cause other programmers to be somewhat mystified and ticked off, resulting in me answering a lot of questions that only a few may be able to understand. This, mixed with my lack of ambition, results in political suicide. I may not know the exact software you need expertise on. Yet, unknown to you, my basic nature can be used to solve these problems.

That's why most of my jobs have been from word of mouth.

Please accept my application for the role of customer service director, which I appreciate may come as a surprise to you given that I was fired from this position last month.

Dear Prospective Employer,

My experience matches the description for Software Developer II for which you advertise.

I enjoy working with people to produce a graphic and redundancy-free architecture that brings developers and users into synchronicity. Since creating a model is essentially the incipient step under the paradigm of top-down programming, an information architect's work is largely cerebral and removed from the tools with which an application is implemented. It involves gathering requirements from the players (users and management). Then, the architect creates a graphic and/or software representation of primary objects and their relationships to other objects.

The format of the graphic representation has never, and will never, change. It is an art form, and I'm very, very good at it. In fact, I would not expect to be long in your employ in that capacity in any case. I already have a highly developed model, which I expect would require only minor 'tweaking' to entirely encompass your need for a management information system.

If you can offer the environment wherein this service is timely, I am interested in exploring further the possibility of working with you.

 I would like to work with a company. First on a small project and then on a larger project. I am an expert at software and debugging. I would like to work in Pennsylvania in one of the cities listed overleaf. I have an RV motor home and can live and work out of this if there is an RV park within twenty miles.

The pros of hiring me, as I see them, are:

Enthusiastic
Problem-solver
Great with people

Possible cons:

No practical experience
Not certified
Quite old

Am to think in exercise to my career of Engineer Electromecânic in kingdom and am to send him my curriculum to some companies among the whom to your company Stay to await the better proposal. Go To send him my curriculum in Portuguese for be one curriculum very technician. Of this form Find good him curriculum be translated in your office, so that him understand well.

I write and speak ingles but for work Very in Portugal this wants use, is one subject of one month in Land for adaptation.

Some doubts contact me.

Dear [insert name of employer],
Although I am quite certain that you have heard or read of me, perhaps even been amazed by some of my ubiquitous work, I feel obliged to inform you that I am the one and only Qathi Gallaher Hart, independently wealthy international woman of mystery and, incidentally, smarter than a monkey.

Yes, that Qathi.

Due to the large number of job offers impending, please label all correspondence 'Employment No. 108/JB4'.

Objective:

So here's the deal. I cannot compete with college degrees and fancy credentials, on paper at least, so I've decided to highlight the best of what I do have to offer.

Previous experience:

Marijuana Dealer and Nefarious Dude, 1999–2004, Nashville & Middle Tennessee

Intuitive understanding of supply-and-demand economics

Good with money

Ran my own delivery service

Had a consistent clientele with high customer satisfaction

Gained intimate access to several very exclusive county jails

Learned a valuable life lesson

References available on request . . . Seriously!

✱ After perusing my resume, I am looking forward to hearing from you soon.

**In closing, let me outline the experiences
I've been able to endure.**

Please, please, please hire me for this job.
I will be waiting by the phone.

Dear Sir/Madam,
I saw your recent advertisement in the *Guardian* newspaper and believe I am the right person for the job. I am a graduate recently returned from a round-the-world adventure and I'm looking for my next challenge.

I am a dynamic figure, often seen scaling walls and crushing ice. I manage time efficiently and occasionally tread water for three days straight. I can pilot bicycles up severe inclines with unflagging speed and cook thirty-minute brownies in twenty minutes. I write award-winning operas over lunch, and on Wednesdays I repair electrical appliances for free. I am an expert in stucco, a veteran in love, and an outlaw in Peru. I am the subject of numerous documentaries.

Using only a hoe and a large glass of water, I once single-handedly defended a small Amazonian village from a horde of ferocious ants. While on holiday in Belgium, I successfully negotiated with a group of terrorists who had seized a small boulangerie. I am an abstract artist, a concrete analyst and a ruthless bookie. Critics worldwide swoon over my original line of corduroy eveningwear. I don't perspire.

I sleep once a week; when I do sleep, I sleep in a chair. On weekends, to let off steam, I participate in full-contact origami. I balance, I weave, I dodge, I frolic, and my bills are all paid. I know the exact location of every food item in the supermarket. I have performed several covert operations with the CIA. Years ago I discovered the meaning of life but forgot to write it down. I breed prize-winning clams. I have won bullfights in San Juan, cliff-diving competitions in Sri Lanka, and chess tournaments at the Kremlin. I have played Hamlet, I have performed open-heart surgery and I have spoken with Elvis.

But I have not yet worked in telemarketing.

APPLICATION FOR EMPLOYMENT

I refer to the recent death of the technical manager at your company and hereby apply for the replacement of the deceased manager.

Each time I apply for a job, I get a reply that there's no vacancy, but in this case I have caught you red-handed and you have no excuse because I even attended the funeral to be sure he was truly dead and buried before applying.

Attached to my letter is a copy of my CV and his death certificate.

PS. As I'm single, I have been questioned by personnel managers in previous interviews about my sexual habits. Weird, but evidently there is a need of explanation. Therefore, I want to let you know that I am heterosexual. I'm only interested in women! I'm absolutely 'normal'. I've got no problems with these questions, and I don't complain about it. We do live in the twenty-first century, after all.

Dear Ladysir!
I would like to present myself the announced webdesigner onto a position! It is included in my long-term plans that he is graphic designer inside a trade let me find a job.

According to my opinion, my school studies, my experiences and it until now two of my year professional practices suitable one do the webdesigner scope of activities onto his filling.

Trust in it, that my letter arouses your interest.

I send it enclosed herewith concerning my curriculum vitae and the reference my works! I wait for their answer!

I would make the work in telework, freelance if may be!!!

Kind regards.

I have mastered every genre, from pointy-shoe-swing kid and glam rockstar, through beat poet and lonesome traveller to cycle-messenger outcast and rockabilly cowboy. I can, and do, shoot from the hip, but only when startled. When I shave, I shave with a straight razor, which I sometimes keep in my left boot. Just in case. I no longer cut my face. I can fix your car, or a flat bicycle tyre. I built my first house entirely from Lego. It's currently on the market, if you're interested.

Sorry, just a quick email to clarify: I misheard you on the phone earlier as asking about my experience with 'paper click' or 'paperclip', which I assumed was some sort of specialist software. I want to stress that, as an online marketing expert, I am indeed familiar with Google pay-per-click.

Yes! I have all the qualifications you
Outline in the job ad on
Ur website. I am
William and
I am a model employee,
Loyal at all costs and also highly
Likable. I have a number of unusual
Hobbies, including code-breaking (and making) and also
Ice-dancing. Please drop me a line
Regarding times for interviews or any written
Exams I might need to sit.
Martin,
Email me!

May I request you to kindly walk the extra mile for us, by passing my bio data to all concerned. You may wonder why I request you to this at our behest and this is due an inner feeling in me which tells that you a woman who believes in human bondage, not to re-mention compassion and kindness.

* For the past three months I have also been living at home with my brother as my parents have gone on holiday for three months as a retirement present. I believe this experience has matured me as a person, as I have had to look after the house, shop and generally do a lot more tasks for myself. This has given me a new outlook on life and what I want to do with my life in the future.

Please find the attached resume, which lists all of my kills.

I am a genius of some renown in certain circles and as such my time is valuable, so I must insist that you come to interview me at my apartment.

✓

I have set up my resume to be sung to the theme tune of *The Brady Bunch*.

✓

To whom it may concern,

Shawn has worked for me for eight years now. During that time he has demonstrated an excellent work ethic, adaptability, team-oriented thinking and excellent knowledge of IT systems.

Shawn is the very definition of a man's man. He once fucked Chuck Norris in the ass; not in a sexual way – it was about dominance and power. He is a level 50 Paladin who still fucks bitches. You may have seen the internet meme Sad Keanu. Shawn is the reason Keanu is sad.

Shawn's physical prowess is unrivalled in the known universe. Shawn does cock push-ups (that's where you lie flat on your stomach and let your boner lift you up). He can only do the one, but I'm told that's all you need.

Shawn is absolutely the most reliable person I've ever known. He is as firm as red clay and as constant as . . . drinking. He's constantly drinking. But Shawn never lets his debilitating alcoholism affect his work ethic. He's always in by 2 p.m. and he routinely stays well past 5 p.m.

Shawn tackles every task he's assigned with tenacity and determination that is unrivalled. He runs ethernet connections with the efficiency of a Nazi death camp. We call Shawn the 'Network Wonderboy'. He configures switches with mind bullets – that's telekinesis. He eats packets and shits frames.

If you choose not to hire Shawn I can say without doubt that he will find your family and make them suffer. They will beg for the sweet release of death long before he grants it.

AT ONE POINT IN TIME DURING IAN'S TWENTY-EIGHT YEARS ON THIS PLANET, HE WAS IN AN AUTOMOBILE ACCIDENT, WHICH PUT A FEW YEARS THERAPY, SOME 'ROLLERCOASTER' EMOTIONAL SOUL JOURNEYS AND A WICKED JOB RESUME, WHICH MOST EMPLOYERS WOULD FROWN UPON, AROUND HIS PRESENT IDENTITY . . . TEN YEARS 'IN THE RUNNING'. HOWEVER, GIVEN THE PRESENT CASH FLOW, VIA THE AMERICAN GOVERNMENT,

CONSISTENCY, BOTH PHYSICALLY AND
EMOTIONALLY, HAVE BEEN REALIZED
AND TOUCHED UPON OVER THE PAST
FEW YEARS. ALL IN ALL, IAN'S
RELATIONSHIP WITH SOCIAL SECURITY
BENEFITS IS GROWING NEAR END IN
RESPONSE TO HIS ACCUMULATED WORK
HISTORY. HENCE, IAN SEES URGENCY,
CLOSURE, SOME FEAR, STRONG DESIRE
AND MATURITY ALL WOVEN INTO THIS
EXPRESSION OF IAN, THE EMPLOYEE, TO
YOU, THE EMPLOYER.

**You hold in your hands the resume of a truly
outstanding candidate!**

Heads up: keep this resume on top of the
stack. Use all the others to heat your house.

**Would you pass up an opportunity to
hire someone like this? I think not.**

Subject: Fine, Don't Fucking Hire Me, You Can't Handle My Shit

What the fuck people! I need a motherfuckin' job, and I have a resume that says I am fucking fit to be your goddamn front desk/administrative assistant. I have applied to a ton of jobs on here, and not one of them responded. WHAT THE FUCK?!

Cover letter? Here's my fucking cover letter!

Now, I'm really low on money, and I'll suck a dick if I have to . . . That's right!

Got a bear in your back yard that keeps eating your garbage? I'll fight that motherfucker and I'll win! Can any other prospective employee say that?! FUCK NO! What did you say? You lost your keys? FUCK IT! I'll shoot the goddamn lock off your door with my laser eyes! That's how bad I need a motherfuckin' job! Your brother is gay and you're not cool with that? I'll de-gay him with reverse butt-sex. Don't believe me?! Then hire me and I'll fucking show you!

OBJECTIVE

I need a motherfuckin' job.

SHIT I HAVE DONE

I invented the moon

Atlantis was around till 1988, but sank when I shot out of my mom's vagina like a silver bullet into a wolverine

I had sex with the Spice Girls

I have prophetic visions of the apocalypse

I created a new genre of dance in which people get so
   into it that radiation waves pulsate off of them. I like to
   call this the microrave
I reverse-engineered a door. I know how it works.
When I was eight a Frisbee flew into my back yard and I
   blew it up with my mind
My brother is the Eiffel Tower
I'm a direct descendant of Beowulf
I can make weapons out of anything – very useful in a
   hostile work environment
I beat my pornography addiction when I was just
   nineteen
I'm proficient in Microsoft Office and Photoshop

RELEVANT WORK EXPERIENCE
GlomGlom Corporation of Evil-Doing
POSITION: front desk/administrative assistant
DUTIES: Setting up sex scandals in which to blackmail
wealthy politicians, forwarding email, burning down the
houses of the poor, loan-sharking, answering phones,
greeting clients in a manner that would frighten most
people.

GreenHate Enterprises
POSITION: Once again, I was a fucking front desk/
administrative assistant
DUTIES: Organizing the dumping of bio-waste into the
ocean, peeing in lakes, digging holes to fill with garbage,
making garbage out of perfectly good and useful items,
filling said holes with said garbage, creating fake facts

about Greenpeace and publishing them on the internet (I am internet-savvy). Good at filing documents of hate.

REFERENCES
Glomgor Evil, GlomGlom Corporation of Evil-Doing
gorlock@peanutbutternipples.com

Sloblor the Muck Monster, GreenHate Enterprises
sloblor@greenhate.com

So, now that you know the real me, are you gonna hire me or not? I would like to remind you that I can make weapons out of anything.
    Sincerely,
    Steve

Remember . . . Anything.

✓

Enclosed is a ruff draft of my resume.

✓

I saw your ad on the information superhighway
and I came to a screeching halt.

* If this resume doesn't blow your hat off, please
return it in the enclosed envelope.

**My fortune cookie said,
'Your next interview will result in a job'
– and I like your company in particular.**

Hi Kelly,
I saw your ad at the job centre the other
day and am wondering if the position is still
available. If so, please could you send me
some more information? I've attached my
CV and covering letter.
   Best wishes,
   Erin Brown

[attachment: photo of Nicolas Cage]

Film roles:	
Devil's Wear Prague	Transit Passenger
American Ginger	Homeless Guy
School for Scurnder	Bench Watcher
The Departed (dir. Martin Scoresissers)	Crack Addict
Enchanged (dir. Tim Burton)	On-looker
Be Kins Rewind (dir. John)	Street Looker

I recently saw your vacancy ad
And think the role sounds really rad.
Here's my resume, have a look and see
I am the master of accountancy.
I own the world of demand and supply
So for this job I will apply.
I've fourteen years beneath my belt
Of tears, hard graft, correctly spelt
Emails (I'm a stickler for good grammar),
But also work well under the hammer:
Deadlines are my raison d'etre.
Am I the guy for this job? You betcha!

Please find attached my son's CV and a letter of
recommendation from me. He is a good lad and you should
definitely hire him.

I note you are the HR Director, so am sending this application to you as a courtesy, though FYI I have already made contact with the actual decision-makers.

If at any point you do not buy this message,
take my cover letter and resume, rip them up,
throw them in the garbage bin and don't forget
to spare me that 'we will keep your resume on
file for three months' crap.

Act I – setting the scene	
I am born (Sagittarius)	1980
I begin to hone my literacy skills	1985
I am elected school prefect and bell monitor	1990

Act II – heightening anticipation	
I achieve higher-than-predicted A Level results (despite debilitating hay fever during exam season – see overleaf)	1998
I graduate with a very high third-class degree (highest in year)	2001
I successfully complete a gap year trip to Thailand etc.	2002

Act III – the drama unfolds	

The next stage of my life adventure is in your hands,
Mr Nelson . . .

✱ I invite you to browse through my resume and offer me an opportunity within your team.

✓

I would be prepared to meet with you at your earliest convenience to discuss what I can do to your company.

✓

Enclosed is my resume for your viewing pleasure.

✓

▶ You are privileged to receive my resume.

✓

Please overlook my resume.

I'm submitting the attached copy of my resume for your consumption.

I've updated my resume so it's more appalling to employers.

Please disregard the attached resume.
It is terribly out of date.

Please see how your enclosed resume will meet the job requirements.

My work history is outlined on my enclosed resume. As you can see there isn't anything too impressive about it.

The interview you schedule will undoubtedly reveal my unmatched talent and suitability for the position.

At the emphatic urging of colleagues, I have consented to applying for your position.

My time is valued at $180/hour, so please bear this in mind when deciding how long to make the interview. I do not offer 'mates' rates'.

✱ Thank you for your time. I look forward to hearing from you in the new future.

But wait . . . there's more!
You get ALL this business knowledge plus a grasp of finance that is second nature.

✖ Thank you for your consideration. Hope to hear from you shorty!

Dear applicant,

I am writing, with regret, to inform you that your name has not been placed on the shortlist of candidates to be invited for interview. I am sorry if this is disappointing for you.

We heard about your previous internet projects and, quite frankly, you scare us.

You may also like to note that calling our head of human resources a 'skank ho' does not gain you any plus points when being shortlisted for a position.

Herbert A. Millington
Chair, Search Committee
412a Clarkson Hall
Whitson University
College Hill MA 34109

Dear Professor Millington,

Thank you for your letter of 16 March. After careful consideration, I regret to inform you that I am unable to accept your refusal to offer me an assistant professor position in your department.

This year I have been particularly fortunate in receiving an unusually large number of rejection letters. With such a varied and promising field of candidates, it is impossible for me to accept all refusals.

Despite Whitson's outstanding qualifications and previous experience in rejecting applicants, I find that your rejection does not meet my needs at this time. Therefore, I will assume the position of assistant professor in your department this August. I look forward to seeing you then.

Best of luck in rejecting future applicants.

Sincerely,
Chris L. Jensen

2.

SEX: YES PLEASE!

Crap CVs

OBJECTIVE

* Now: Get the job. Later: Keep the job.

* Be important.

* To work for any pay.

* To utilize my creative talent in a mundane office.

* To be able to make banana bread and share it with co-workers.

* To hopefully associate with a millionaire one day.

* To claw my way to the top using any means necessary.

* To secure a position as a front office.

* To wake up in the morning and shout, 'I can't wait to get to work!'

* To have my skills and ethics challenged on a daily basis.

OBJECTIVE

* To work in a challenging environment that allows me to use my imaginatiation.

* To obtain a position that will enable me to utilize my professional skills and knowledge in a capacity that demonstrates me intelligence.

* To become a billionier.

* To begin my post-graduate career in an insignificant, entry-level position that will provide me with income.

* To find a job as a paralegal!

* To obtain an entry-level position after I get my beachler's degree.

* To make money, and be the camel tha t squeezes through the eye of the needle.

* To obtain a position with the skills in hence the skills I already inquire.

OBJECTIVE

* To grow with a company that maintains a FIRST CLASS culture.

* To broaden my computer skills and decrease my use of antacids.

* To mature in the field of human behaviour.

* To be employed at a wage above the poverty level.

* To obtain a position that will allow me to utilize my strengths and reinforce my weaknesses.

* To obtain a position that will exploit my potential.

* To make dough.

* To obtain a position within an organization in which both my fashion and administrative experience can be of great detriment.

OBJECTIVE

* To secure a position in a large firm as receptionist, computer operator, manager, owner or accounts receivable clerk.

* To learn new skills and gain training which will help me develop my new business.

* To be a fair and just ruler and bring your company to new heights, or whatever.

* 2 get dat $$$$.

* To work for someone who is not an alcoholic with three DUIs, like my current employer.

* If I were in a position to be picky,
  I wouldn't be applying here in the first place.

* My aim is to become a marketing director for a large international company once I have graduated from university.

* Desired role: Employee.

OBJECTIVE

* Objective: Reception.

* Objective: A job.

* Objective: [Click here and type your objective]

* Career objection: To maximum my skills.

* EZ $$$$$$$$$$$$$$$$$

* A career on the information supper highway.

* A great management team that has patents with its workers.

* A position that allows me to keep my sanity.

* I promise to make your store 10000000000000000000 oooooooooooooooooooooooooooo dollars, and if not I will give you permission to execute me.

OBJECTIVE

* I want to be an astronaut, but I think working in a call centre will help me gain confidence for talking to mission control from space.

* I am seeking a permanent position to get out of debt.

* I am looking for a challenging career where there is scope for ample demonstration because I am always on the lookout for a positive and bigger outlook, currency and ideas that thrive on imagination, passion, boundless curiosity and rigorous thinking.

* Desire a career as a trainee.

* I am sicking and entry-level position.

* I am looking for a proffreading position.

* Position desired: Profreader.

* Target position: Missionary.

OBJECTIVE

* Eager to learn innate abilities.

* Student today. Vice president tomorrow.

* My plan is to become Overlord of the Galaxy!

* It is my professional objective to obtain a position that allows me to make use of my commuter skills.

* I'm looking for a challenging, fun, fulfilling job and a paycheck. (If the pay is good, I'll get the fun and fulfillment outside of work.)

* My goal in life is to win the Nobel Peace Prize through the next big business: global psychological reconstruction.

* I would love to work abroad – Bali, Maldives, etc.

* I am anxious to use my exiting skills.

* I am dedicating my future to socialisticly unite the third world countries through the use of media.

OBJECTIVE

* To quote the great [candidate's own name]: 'It's time to knuckle down, get a haircut and a proper job.' These days, as there's scant requirement for a pirate with a heart of gold, I'm shopping out my more creative talents.

* I would like to work for a company that is very lax when it comes to tardiness.

* Ten-year goal: total obliteration of sales and federal income taxes and tax laws.

* Personal goal: to hand-build a classic cottage from the ground up using my father-in-law.

* My ideal company: somewere were if i wanted i could work my way up to a better job a place to meet different people make new friends

* I am looking for a company that is driven to excellent.

OBJECTIVE

* I don't have any particular ambitions for advancement, as long as I am paid a lot more in five years' time.

* The jobs I'm interested in are [insert job description here].

* My dream is to be an astronomer, but since I possess literally zero training in astronomy I am currently looking for work as a stockbroker.

* I am looking for a change of scenery.

* I am an accomplished executive assistant who is ready to become the executive.

* I want to play a major part in watching a company advance.

* I vow to fulfill the goals of the company as long as I live.

OBJECTIVE

* i beg to state that i have dream in my eyes to decorate this world with my creativity.

* Charming analyst with GSOH and PhD WLTM seriously hot HR Supervisor for interviews, salary negotiations and possibly more.

* I'm extremely motivated to find a position where I can apply my love of interpersonal communication to multifaceted colleagues.

* It is my desire to develop and generate the revolving scheme to filter to the consuming public in.

* I expect the position to pay commissary to that of its value, as well as to the performance completed.

* i am graduated from height school and i am currently seeking a full time job in aprofessional environment i am knowledgeable in word, office power point ext. i would prefer to work mornings.

* I'm looking manly for a retail role.

OBJECTIVE

* I have searched far and wide for an employer who is energetically inclined.

* Long-term plants: to pursue my master's degree.

* I seek challenges that test my mind and body, since the two are usually inseparable.

* Assertive, self-motivated and goal-oriented individual seeks a position that utilizes my computer training and experience and/or bartending skills.

* I AM INTERESTING TO WORK AS A TRANEE ENGINEER.

* I am looking forward to working in a distinct and dynamic environment, where I can intensify my engineering flairs.

* I prefer to work with people that can inspire me, both creatively and spiritually (although I am not a religious person).

OBJECTIVE

* I am seeking a second job to supplement my income and support my shopping habit.

* I believe in what studies have shown: that nap times each day increase employee productivity. I wish to work for a company that provides for this.

* Goals: I want to increase my goals.

* When my situation allows, I would like to get a puppy.

ABOUT ME

* Name: Nora (Nora is my full, legal name. I have a one-word name).

* Preferred name/nickname: Phone Book.

* Contact: hottt_shizzle@.com

* Emergency contact number: 999

* Married 20 years; own a home, along with a friendly mortgage company.

* Marital status: Repeatedly. Children: various.

* Marital status: Single. Unmarried. Uninvolved. Nada.

* Marital status: Unknown

* Sex: Occasionally

* Contact: nicksupershag@.com

ABOUT ME

* Health: Trick knee. Impairs only hard labour, such as playing basketball.

* I am in excellent health, except for ingrown toenail.

* Weight: 165 pounds (without coins in my pockets).

* Sex: A couple of times a month, depending on the wife's mood and menstrual cycle.

* Personal: Classic Capricorn.

* Contact: pornstar69@.com

* Sex: Yes please!

* Contact: batfacedgirl@.com

* About me: Highly attractive.

* I'm twenty-nine years old but have the facial hair of a thirteen-year-old.

ABOUT ME

* Emergency contact number: Depends on nature of emergency, but 911 for medical or criminal disasters and 432-8100 if you need to talk to my mother.

* Summary: I am a strawberry/dirty blonde of average height and weight (BMI 23), with greenish-blue eyes and eight years' teaching experience.

* Contact: lazysod@.com

* Marital status: Celibate.

* I am 5 foot 9 inches with green eyes and ears of approximately 3 inches in length.

* Contact: shakinmybootay@.com

* Marital status: Single (!)

* Sex: Not yet. Still waiting for the right person.

* Strengths: Really good at Lego.

ABOUT ME

* Weaknesses: Bullets.

* Contact: hotsexyluv@.com

* Married, eight children. Prefer frequent travel.

* I am fit as a fiddle with only chronic anxiety and recurring skin complaints on my immediate family's list of medical conditions. (cousin has diabetes but maybe not relevant?)

* Age: Sixty-three (but fit as a forty-nine-year-old cripple)

* I weigh 10 stone 3 pounds (10 stone 2 after my morning coffee).

* Contact: idontstealofficesupplies@.com

* I'm sixteen, I'm pregnant and I can do anything.

ABOUT ME

* I am in excellent dental and gum health and have had just two fillings in my lifetime thus far.

* Weaknesses: Suffer from prickly heat in summer.

* Contact: dubious_dude@.com

* Icons I follow: Mahatma Gandhi (ethics), Beyoncé (style, business).

* Please follow me on Twitter and then I'll DM you my real name and contact details.

PERSONAL ATTRIBUTES

* I am an earnest and enthusiastic leading man available for auditions. I just finished playing a rapist in a film.

* Hard worker, dedicated etc.

* I have the more than the high levels of energy than required for any job.

* I am a marketing superstar with a 'never settle for the best' attitude.

* I am a great team player I am.

* I am a wedge with a sponge taped to it. My purpose is to wedge myself into someone's door and absorb as much as possible.

* Most positive attribute: Chatty.

* Jimmy likes to ski. Jimmy has three years' programming experience. Jimmy knows HTML code and Java.

PERSONAL ATTRIBUTES

* Responsibility makes me nervous.

* I have guts, drive, ambition and heart, which is probably more than a lot of the drones that you have working for you.

* I am a 'neat nut' with a reputation for being hardnosed. I have no patience for sloppywork, carelessmistakes and theft of companytime.

* I am loyal and know when to keep my big trap shut.

* I am a confident person because of the few individuals like you that I plan to befriend.

* I am on my third incarnation at present.

* I limit important relationships to people who want to do what I want them to do.

* I have a great deal of integrity and will not steal office supplies for home use.

PERSONAL ATTRIBUTES

* Strong work ethic, attention to detail, team player, self-motivated, attention to detail.

* Detailed-oriented saleman.

* I prefer a fast-paste work environment.

* I am a former surfer turned receptionist.

* Tell us a little about yourself: I am 6 feet 3 inches tall.

* Horse-like laugh (optional).

* My intensity and focus are at inordinately high levels, and my ability to complete projects on time is unspeakable.

* I am a scholar of life and mishaps.

* Emit pleasant aroma(s).

PERSONAL ATTRIBUTES

* I am a BOSS at working. No pun intended.

* I believe in the quote 'who cares wins'.

* My ruthlessness terrorizes the competition and can sometimes offend.

* Excellent memory; strong math aptitude; excellent memory; effective management skills and very good at math.

* I am quick to lean.

* I am relatively intelligent, obedient and as loyal as a puppy.

* I am often told by others, in the manifold spheres of my activities, that there is a mystic in what I do.

* I am internally motivated – a warrior type, though I enjoy yoga very much.

PERSONAL ATTRIBUTES

* A lover of all things green, though allergic to avocados and somewhat intolerant to kiwi.

* I am a silver-tongued serpent who can talk anyone into anything.

* I have an excellent track record, although I am not a horse.

* The eye-catcher about me is that I'm definitely a people person!

* I expect the unexpected so nothing shocks me.

* I perform my job with effortless efficiency, effectiveness, efficacy and expertise.

* Outstanding worker; flexible 24 hours a day, 7 days a week, 365 days a year.

* Raised by a father who was a member of a military special operations group, I'm a man who doesn't intimidate easily.

PERSONAL ATTRIBUTES

* In my next life, I will be a professional backup dancer or a rabbi.

* I am not pedantic but embrace any occasion to nurture my edification and I champion the prodigious accolades of verisimilitude expertise your clients desire.

* Was an unhappy, drifting bachelor until I met my lovely wife, Anne, whose work ethic and inspiring nature made me the responsible person I am today.

* I work furiously.

* I think outside of the box (without even realizing it).

* I am getting to my goal, slowly but surly.

* I am eternally aspiring to conquer myself in everything I do and every elevation I gain.

* My infectious enthusiasm makes me a vital ass to any company.

PERSONAL ATTRIBUTES

* The colours red, blue and lavender are those that I identify with the most. I feel they accurately describe my personality.

* Not only am I creative, I am a very hardworking. Give me a project and I don't stop until it is finished or I am told to.

* A flaw that I must point out because it even bothers me is that I am impatient. I hate waiting, but then again, who does?

* I am a motivated, self-igniting person.

* I am an all-rounder with a strong breath.

* Everything I do must be done in Safeway.

* I don't consummate alcohol.

* I am self-discipline.

PERSONAL ATTRIBUTES

* I am a perfectionist with a keen I for details.

* I am a tiger when needed, but otherwise a pussycat.

* I have a broad knowledge of accounting procedures. I am a quick learner who is self-motivated and flexible. But above all, I am a jobaholic!

* Much like the mighty Dyson vacuum cleaner, I am an innovative whirlwind in attractive packaging. It is my calling to be borne along the corridors and into the meeting rooms of your company, sucking up every atom of creativity and vision.

* I am challenged creatively and professionally on all levels.

* I am a hustler.

* Excellent at people-oriented positi9ons and organizional problem solving.

* I'm a lean, mean accounting machine.

PERSONAL ATTRIBUTES

* I have a wonderful son and two delicious grandchildren.

* I never take anything for granite.

* Dynamic, solutions-oriented professional with over twenty years' teaching experience in torturing.

* I was made to be the perfect employee.

* I'm worth investigating.

* Eager beaver, ready to know it all.

* I am a loyal and dedicated worker. Please feel free to contact me on my office direct line.

* I have not yet been abducted by aliens.

* I won't perform well under pressure.

* I offer mediocrity at its best.

PERSONAL ATTRIBUTES

* I enjoy working closely with customers, and my pleasant demeanour helps them feel comfortable and relaxed – not afraid.

* I am enthusiastic and people like me.

* I eat computers for lunch.

* I am meticulate about derails.

* I can play well with others.

* I would like to assure you that I am a hardly working person.

* I am a workhorse of the first degree. But unlike the lowly workhorse, I do not come with blinkers.

* I'm able to bring nobility to any firm.

* I can describe myself in three words: committed, hard-working and very strategic thinking.

PERSONAL ATTRIBUTES

* I am a pit bull when it comes to analysis.

* I procrastinate, especially when the task is unpleasant.

PREVIOUS EXPERIENCE

* I have had sex jobs to date.

* I am a sr DBA with seven yrs of exp avl on wk's notice.

* Tattoo assistant.

* Hymen checker on Australian sheep farm.

* Title at previous employment: Mr.

* Previous job: Plumber. Reason for leaving: Couldn't plumb.

* I spent four seasons as the rump end of a pantomime cow.

PREVIOUS EXPERIENCE

★ Wrapping gifts at the hospital
★ Wrapping gifts at the mall
★ Wrapping gifts elsewhere

---

* Duties: Touring children around and giving them coke.

* As for leadership experience, I have risen swiftly up the military ranks in Battle World Four, now commanding eight previously rival warrior clans and a horde of fire vampires.

* I have had experience in logic programming, basic software creation, bear wrestling, and am fluent in Java.

* My experience in food preparation and customer service would make me the most perfect addition to the Chicken Cottage family.

* I worked at McDonald's in the holidays and cleaned up after every shit.

PREVIOUS EXPERIENCE

* 1983–present: World-class bro.

* Previous job: Owned a small business. Reason for leaving: Got fired.

* Management experience: Dungeon Master.

* Wholly responsible for two (2) failed financial institutions.

* Duties: Filing, billing, printing and coping.

* 2008–present: Chairman and Communications Director at Yale University (Chess Society).

* I am a one-year-old marketing executive.

* 03/96–02/00: Most of the jobs and the dates at witch I worked I am unable to recall.

PREVIOUS EXPERIENCE

* Hired to lead a team of eight in a four-year project to implement innovative efficiency systems in the data management sector.
  (This work was not completed.)

* Duties: I was charged with implementing a plan to totally dominate 38 per cent of the market.

* The idea was a gift from God, so unfortunately I am not able to share my methodology with you here.

* An accomplished professional with deliberate experience in project management.

* Job title: Night Stalker.

* My last two places of employment closed down while I was working there.

* Performed brain-wave tests, 1879–1981.

PREVIOUS EXPERIENCE

2006–7: Clothes store accesory's dept.

Well, Basically i had my own dept. because i was full-time in the dept. everyone else quit because the sais i was challenging i put the buzzers on the purses stocked them organized the earings/braclets and etc.

---

* I am very experienced in all modern databases and online security systems (my boyfriend is kind of a hacker).

* I have a lifetime's worth of technical expertise (I wasn't born – my mother simply chose 'eject child' from the special menu).

* Spent several years in the United States Navel Reserve.

* Written communication: Thirteen years. Verbal communication: Sixteen years.

* Sold fireworks for two weeks.

PREVIOUS EXPERIENCE

* Two years as a blackjack and baccarat dealer. Strong emphasis on customer relations – a constant challenge considering how much money people lose and how angry they can get.

* I am quite experienced with the McDonald's menu.

* Duties: Provided snakes and lunch for kids.

1999: Starbucks

⋆ Made, consumed and sold addictive substances to minors and adults

⋆ Translated confusing customer orders into concrete company jargon

⋆ Routinely served as the face of a multinational corporation to the public

⋆ Distributed free doughnuts to all members of the DC police force

* Worked with my dad building things. Worked with my mum cleaning the house.

PREVIOUS EXPERIENCE

* I spent one summer as an intern helping to construct the International Space Station and was sent to supervise the process in laboratories around the globe.

* Nursing, housekeeping, chef, teacher, bio-hazard clean-up, fight referee, taxi driver, secretary, tailor, personal shopping assistant and therapist (AKA: mother).

* My main expertise is in commercial crayfishing.

2004–6: Cock/Food Prep/Pizza Maker

★ Cocking Sauce's, Pizza's, Pasta's
★ Cocking for up to 150+ people

1996–present: Business Incorporated, Vice President of Impressive Business Dealings

★ Outsourcing and in-buying
★ Overseeing important industry
★ Burning the midnight oil

PREVIOUS EXPERIENCE

1992–1995: *The Newspaper*, reporter

★ Wrote lots of articles
★ Took excellent photographs
★ Won Puletsur Prize and donated it to charity

2001–2002: Prisoner

Duties included lashing out hysterically, tossing prisoners' salads, throwing flaming toilet paper and occasionally working in the kitchen.

1999–2000: Magazine correspondent

Corresponded with other correspondents over drinks, watched girls urinate through heating duct in bathroom.

1998–1999: UFO abductee

Duties included being snatched from my home in the middle of the night, taken to an alien laboratory and forced to eat cold cuts.

1992–1995: Self-employed bench-warmer

Talked to self while sitting on the park bench, fed dead pigeons to other pigeons.

PREVIOUS EXPERIENCE

1990–1995: Self-employed son of a bitch

Duties included borrowing stuff and never returning it, picking fights and pursuing my friends' wives.

---

* Experience: None really, but please allow me to articulate the many reasons why I think my minimum-wage work history is extremely relevant and has adequately prepared me for this job.

* All the jobs I've had previously have been boring and drudgerous and disheartening. I should state I was not bad at them.

* Duties: Bleaching, pot-washing, window-cleaning, mopping etc.

EXPERIENCE

2007: Lost virginity.
2008: Graduated from University of Miami (Biology); statistics teaching assistant; managed 5+ member teams.
2009: Data analyst; managed database of 3,500+ agents; almost tricked into marriage.

PREVIOUS EXPERIENCE

2010: Company execs escape after bankrupting company; took time off to travel the world; experimented with soft-core drugs.

2011: Internet search consultant; full-time Wikipedia reader.

2012: Will carry company to promised land on my strong back.

---

* I served as assistant sore manager.

* I have exhaustive experience in manufacturing.

* Work history: Bum. Abandoned belongings and led nomadic lifestyle.

* I like slipping and sliding around behind the counter and controlling the temperature of the food.

* My experience in horticulture is well-rooted.

* Frequent lecturer. Largest Audience: 1,351. Standing ovations: 5. Number of audience questions: 30.

PREVIOUS EXPERIENCE

* I held sex positions as a manager.

* Duties: I worked with employees.

* I dont have any expereince related to Journalism background. Iam a fast learner.

* In my misspent youth I repeatedly evaded the law as a pickpocket, drug dealer, burglar and internet fraudster, so I know I have the makings of an expert policeman.

* Duties: LOL, doodies!

* 2010–12: Sales rep. Satisfying customers and making sure customers are satisfied.

* Watered, groomed and fed the family dog for years.

* Ten years' experience in financail budgiting and transactions rigistering.

PREVIOUS EXPERIENCE

* 2004–8: Marketing assistant. When writing and editing actor bios for theatre playbills, I had to explain to small-town actors that no one really cared that they had the starring role in things like Mrs Smith's third-grade class rendition of Peter and the Pumpkin Patch.

* In no particular order, I've served stints as a marketing director, poet, book-keeper, honky-tonk DJ, bartender, teacher, line cook, office manager and wrangler of chaos.

* My current job involves looking at children aged two to four.

* Duties: Advised women on tampons and proper hygiene.

* I have one year's experience in the world-famous telecommunications industry.

* Duties: Created brilliant presentations.

PREVIOUS EXPERIENCE

* My contributions to product launches were based on dreams I had had.

* I was previously employed by my mother, until she moved house without informing me.

* Duties: Directed $25 million anal shipping and receiving operations.

* More than seven (8) years of general experience, of which more than four (5) years is in analysing, designing and testing client/server applications.

* 1998–2001: Restaurant manager. Cleaned and supervised employees.

* Duties: Word processing, phones and running errors.

* My previous job provided me with a strong look into network administration, but no actual training.

* Computer games tester (still reigning Tetris champion).

PREVIOUS EXPERIENCE

* My friends call me R-E-G-G-I-E, and that sums up my work experience.

* Responsibilities included recruiting, screening, interviewing and executing final candidates.

* Extensive background in public accounting. I can also stand on my head!

* Operated ghost house; understudy for grim reaper.

* The blue-chip ultra-corporate experience I gained was invaluable if not irreplaceable.

* Part-time office work, when I had time and work.

* I was involved in every aspect of the business, including office administration, customer service and cadaver preparation.

* Short stints with various fast-food restaurants.

PREVIOUS EXPERIENCE

* Currently unemployed due to self-inflicted toe sprain.

* Very experienced with out-house computers.

* I have driving experience with all sorts of cars: minivan, roadster, saloon, estate etc.

* Experienced supervisor, defective with both rookies and seasoned professionals.

* Experience: Assistant Professor – thought-accounting and finance.

* Duties: Supervised employees, scheduled shifts, maintained financial records and ate pizza three times a day.

* Worked successfully on a team of one.

* My duties included cleaning the restrooms and seating the customers.

PREVIOUS EXPERIENCE

* Two summers as a 'customer service representative' at The Blue Orchid (a gentlemen's club).

* Duties: Revolved customer problems and inquiries.

2004–2006: Supermarket sales assistant

i as a online shopper .our dept,its called grossory online.i m a shopper,n do all the work in absence of supervisour n manager.managing the dept well.i.e doing paper work,making sure tht we have enough shoppers n drivers 2 make sure the deliverys is on time,allocating vans to drivers n work to shoppers accordingly.

* 1988–1993: Air Hostess, Royal Air Force.

* Duties: Provided service for old man for check they are still alive or not.

PREVIOUS EXPERIENCE

* Planned ambitious corporate facility at £3 million over budget.

* Duties: When providing childcare for clients, I fed the children and changed dippers.

* 2009: Pizza delivery. Took delivery orders over the phone. Great delivery service. Great delivery service.

* Handled horrendous projects that no one else wanted to do (especially major filing).

* Duties: Truck driver. Drove a truck.

* I was the only employee of a very small distribution company.

* Duties: Helping people with their clothes, greeting people, ringing people out.

* Was soul IT support for total of 100 users.

PREVIOUS EXPERIENCE

* Duties included deposing trash at the end of each working day.

* Provided quality service in each job, starting with my first paper route at age nine.

* As an administrative professional, I coordinate meetings, make travel arrangements and assist security staff with badgering.

* Duties: Responsible for drug abuse, alcohol and antisocial behaviour.

* I have eight jears fo experience.

* Previous experience: Self-employed – a fiasco.

* I work in the store's men's department, stalking shirts and pants.

PREVIOUS EXPERIENCE

* I am proficient in various conflict resolution scenarios, notably Arctic warfare.

* Duties: Provide custer service.

* Worked in a consulting office where I carried out my own accountant.

* I have worked with restraints for the past two years.

* Duties: Answer phones, file papers, respond to customer e-mails, take odors.

* Was brought in by British company to take control of Belgium.

2009: Cosmetics store supervisor

★ Spent time looking at girls
★ Mixed spray-on hair dye in shampoo bottles
★ Made racist comments to customers when they weren't listening and gave them the finger when they weren't looking

PREVIOUS EXPERIENCE

2007: Clothing store customer service advisor

- ★ Got rid of annoying customers who were a pain in the ass
- ★ Regularly put the clock forward twenty minutes to get time off early
- ★ Learned to dress up as the ideal Asian bride in front of the giant mirror after closing time
- ★ Regularly put own phone number in men's coats but didn't get a single date
- ★ (I am an ugly guy who specializes in 'before' photos in multiple infomercials).

---

* Duties: Whilst working in this role, I had intercourse with a variety of people.

* Size of current employer: Very tall – probably over 6 foot 5 inches.

* I supervise employees with the iron fist!

* Whilst working in the hairdressers I had to deal with a lot of old biddies.

PREVIOUS EXPERIENCE

* Brought in a man who made balloon animals to entertain the team.

* I have extensive experience with foreign accents.

1999: Wendy's cashier

* Successfully handled money
* Received money from customers
* Successfully issued the correct amount of change back to the customers

---

* I have many tears' experience in sales.

* Previous role: Salesperson (thirty-one hours only).

* I worked with Mr Imran Khan (Former Pakistan cricket player) in his campaign for cancer.

* I have a wide variety of skills and experience, some of which I have taken for granted and cannot readily recall.

PREVIOUS EXPERIENCE

* Four years' experience in accounting (twenty-eight in dog years).

* This last position enabled me to hone my copyediting and prootreading skills.

2010–Present: McDonald's Restaurant Ltd.

★ Supervising staff
★ Cashing up
★ Cashier
★ Customer service – selling stock
★ Managing the store-opening/closing up
★ Dealing with customers queries
★ Authorizing refunds/exchanges
★ Acquiring knowledge of all new products

* Duties: Made coffee (early Java experience).

PREVIOUS EXPERIENCE

10/02–08/05: God

Oversaw and maintained creation, chaos and stability of the entire universe. Forced to resign due to conflict of opinion with human race with respect to the flavour of car wax.

---

* I have extensive contract negation experience.

* I was brought in as a turnaround consultant to help turn the company around.

* Duties: Answer phones, file papers, respond to customer e-mails, take odors.

* Current job: Arcade attendant. I count tickets. I shred tickets. I try my best to convince customers that giant SpongeBob SquarePants toys are worth the 100 bucks they wasted on arcade games.

* Employer: Myself; received pay raise for high sales.

PREVIOUS EXPERIENCE

* Responsibilities included checking customers out.

* Duties: Maintained files and reports, did data processing, cashed employees' paychecks.

* Experienced in all faucets of accounting.

* I have eight years' experience of managing cabin crew in a pressurized environment.

* Current job: I am not at liberty to disclose details of my work due to its sensible nature.

ACHIEVEMENTS

* Consistently tanked as top sales producer for new accounts.

* In middle school I won the rosette for Best Toothpick Bridge.

* In my gap year I taught troubled inner-city youths to find new hope through Pilates.

* Nominated for prom queen.

* Attained third place in Miss Moose River 1982.

* I literally 'climbed the ladder' at this organization.

* Completed eleven years of high school.

* Awards: My last client called me a god, so that was award enough.

* I was promoted to Shit Leader and responsible for a team of engineers.

ACHIEVEMENTS

* I came first in the school long-distance race.

* I became one of the first members of the geometry club after it had been without members for four years in a row, and I blew new life into it.

* I performed a series of impossible miracles and swiftly rose up the metaphorical ladder.

* As a salesman I smashed numbers through the roof and electrified my team into producing their best ever results.

* I gained a new perspective on life after surviving a bite from a deadly aquatic animal.

* I designed and developed a stapler that was capable of stapling up to thirty sheets of paper in 2004.

* Last week I signed a quite substantial international deal that my team won even after charging the client considerably more than our own colleagues in other countries!

ACHIEVEMENTS

* I was named Time magazine's Person of the Year for 2006.

* I am proud to say I only ever liked disco for a few months in the Eighties.

* Instrumental in ruining entire operation for a Midwest chain store.

* The Marines is and probably will be the biggest accomplishment I've ever had, even though I wasn't able to join.

* Raised over £6,000 for charity by sitting on a commode.

* Overcame procrastination.

* Coordinated 1998 sales fair, and lost £75.

* I have a current passport.

* My mother once interviewed a bunch of famous serial killers.

ACHIEVEMENTS

- ★ Forty-eight-hour porno marathon
- ★ Can count well over 100
- ★ Successfully conquered skin rash in 'special area'

* Homecoming Prom Prince, 1984.

* Professional achievements: Have flown on a corporate jet.

* Consistently contributed to the success and failure of projects.

* I trained my cat to use and flush a human toilet.

* Achievements: Having an Asian girlfriend.

* I invented Gmail before Google thought of it.

* I single-handedly organized a massive sponsored camp-out on the school playing field to raise money for charity, but sadly the police got involved after an

ACHIEVEMENTS

'incident' at the nearby McDonald's (not my fault) and the whole thing ended in complete disaster.

* Accomplishments: I accidentally invented AIDS.

* I voted for Hitler fourteen times in a row.

* Being sober.

* Successfully putting daughter to bed over 100 times.

SPECIAL SKILLS

* Catlike reflexes. Now you see me, *meow* you don't.

* I bake good cakes for people's birthdays.

* I am bilingual in three languages.

* I am an expert in persuading people – professionally, socially, sexually – using just the power of my words.

* I am great with the pubic.

* I am a very determined and hardworking individual whom pays extraordinary attention to detail.

* I am detailed-oriented.
  I am deetail-oriented.
  I am detali-oriented.
  I am detail-orientad.
  I am extremely detailoriented.

* I prohibit excellent written and oral communication skills.

SPECIAL SKILLS

* Able to function without emergency oxygen at 33,000 feet.

* I can juggle and use power tools.

* Fluency in five languages has given me an international personality.

* Strong ability to meet deadlines (just in time).

* Experienced with numerous office machines and can make great lattes.

* Technical equipment: Human brain 1.0.

* Ability to work over pressure.

* Languages: Fluent in languages.

* I am a natural winner. Even before I was born I won a competition against a few million other spermatozoids.

SPECIAL SKILLS

* My English fluent.

* I can tyoe without looking at thekeyboard.

* I come fully armed with the powers of verbal seduction.

* I am quick of wit and eagled of eye.

* My attendance is exemplary – just fourteen sick days in the whole of 2009.

* Special skills: Thyping.

* I am quick at typing: about 30 wpm per, 45 wpm with strong coffee.

* Typing speed: 756 wpm.

* I am a perfectionist and rarely if if ever forget details.

SPECIAL SKILLS

* Good people skills, except when people get on my nerves. Which is hardly ever – no more than once every ten or twelve minutes.

* I host a superlative proficiency for resolving complex systematic problems. I have pedagogic expertise conducting sales, and I can be quickly utilized as an assiduous, visceral and proactive problem solver.

* Versatile toes.

* I'm try-lingual.

* Technical skills: Flappy Bird level 58.

* I host a superlative proficiency for resolving complex systematic problems. I have pedagogic expertise conducting sales, and I can be quickly utilized as an assiduous, visceral and proactive problem solver.

* Very fast metabolism.

SPECIAL SKILLS

* Brainstorming on innovative ideas that take into consideration demographics, target markets, advertising strategies and shifts in the economy that have a direct impact on consumer buying trends, as well as the influences that drive those changes, is one of my many strengths.

* Gator hunting.

* Possibly psychic.

* Can pay attention to two details.

* Can calculate on command.

* One of the UK's top mountaineers once praised my stamina.

* Languages: Twenty-three years of fluency in English.

* I am a bomb expert.

SPECIAL SKILLS

* Can do excellent triceratops impersonation.

* Really good at picking locks.

* Not a child molester.

* I always staple at a 45° angle to the corner of the paper.

* I don't need maternity leave like a woman. I don't go shopping on my lunch breaks like a woman. I don't have mood swings once a month like a woman. I don't gossip about people LIKE A WOMAN.

* I am able to say my ABCs backwards in under five seconds.

* Computer skills: Tiger Woods Golf.

* Riding a bicycle.

SPECIAL SKILLS

* Skills: Yeah, I got 'em.

* Creativity, bravery, arrogance, cleverness and honesty.

* Special skills: Good with money and working on own initiative.

* Reason for leaving: Fired for stealing.

* Can summon sea creatures within 15 feet of water (boiling or room temperature).

* Walking – I am extremely good at this.

* Reliance on God for optimal results.

* Chivalry.

* I'm an editorial samurai.

* I provide excellent costume service.

SPECIAL SKILLS

* Languages: I know English and :-)

* Yes, I am proficient in using the software you mention. (I assume – haven't downloaded it yet but am very good at computers, can do graphs, internet and so on.)

* I don't have any programming skills so you will know better than me whether I am suitable for the job.

* I possess a number of secret skills that will blow your mind.

* I am not a numbers person, but my interpersonal skills make me an engaging accountant.

* I am fluent in the internet.

* Not bad at 'sexy' dancing.

* Can eat a LOT in one sitting. Oh, and I also Moonwalk quite well.

SPECIAL SKILLS

* Want to know how many ways I can communicate? All the ways. That's right. Need me to say stuff? I can do that. Want me to type some stuff? Done. Talk on the phone? Call me right now and guess what: I'LL ANSWER SO POLITELY IT WILL AMAZE YOU.

* I can hold my breath for two minutes.

* I am pretty handy with a hatchet.

* Demonstrated ability in multi-tasting.

* I speak English and Spinach.

* Additional skills: I am a Notary Republic.

* There's almost no task that I can't complete given an opportunity. I taught myself to drive and cook. I knock out a cracking rendition of Kenny Rogers' 'The Gambler'. I am the best at everything I do. I think laterally. My greatest pleasure is to explore the unseen world that exists in the dreams of the everyday.

SPECIAL SKILLS

* Hiding.

* Technical skills: I can type wicked fast! Also texting.

* I often use a laptap.

* I bring doughnuts on Fridays.

* Ability to meet deadlines while maintaining composer.

* Technical experience: Stapler.

* Grate communication skills.

* Able to whistle while pretending to drink water at the same time.

* Insufficient writing skills, mentally slower than I used to be. If I am not one of the best, I will go on and find another opportunity.

SPECIAL SKILLS

* Loving towards the elderly and hired help.

* I type 102 wpm as of 9 a.m. on 3 January 2006.

* Grew an impressive vegetable garden.

* My technical skills will literally take your breath away.

* Fluent in English. Also I have been heard muttering Gibberish in my sleep.

* Fluent in Fench.

* Technical skills: Experience using ATMs.

* Technical skills: PlayStation 2.

* Getting stuck items out of vending machines.

* Very high learning ability and simple thinking.

SPECIAL SKILLS

* I wok well with computers.

* Computer literate and excellent experience in operating Windows.

* I have x-tremely good communication skillz.

* Can drink ten beers without getting too drunk.

* Fluid in French.

* I have demonstrable analytical and problem-solving skills. As a child I always enjoyed building jigsaw puzzles and was always determined to find the missing piece.

* I am able to show up at the office on time, not only during the first week but even after a year of employment.

* I speak several languages, and I am very handsome.

SPECIAL SKILLS

* I am very used to working with thigh schedules.

* Read, write, speak and think fluently in German, French and Spanish.

* Languages: Exposure to German for two years, but many words are inappropriate for business.

* Strengths: Impersonal skills.

* I have superior internet skills.

* Microst word, excel and power point. Mulitaks person, public speaking and surveying.

* I can sort of make coffee.

* Goog at computer work.

* I am a very capapable proofreader.

SPECIAL SKILLS

* I have spent ten years refining my edititing skills.

* Through my career experiences I have become inept at communication skills.

HOBBIES

* None at present.

* Karaoke. I thrive on the confidence that karaoke gives me.

* Gossiping.

* Most of my free time is spent getting sunburned at motorcross races.

* Rabid sports fan.

* Donating blood. Fifteen gallons so far!

* I played football in primary school.

* Shot at the local gun club.

* Playing with Boy Scouts.

* Liposuction.

HOBBIES

* i like to have a laugh wid me mates.

* I love anything to do with radio waves and magic.

* Balloon animals are a passion of mine.

* Bungee jumping, paragliding, cliff diving and customer service.

* In my spare time I restore old vintage clocks and antique Dutch violins.

* I love reading (particularly 3D 'Magic Eye' series).

* Doing various activities with my girlfriend.

* Writing. I have one or two great ideas for film scripts, though I appreciate you are not advertising for that.

* I rank eightieth in the world of yo-yoing.

HOBBIES

* Interests: Having a good time.

* I have unsuccessfully raised a dog.

* Avoiding my wife.

* Playing with my two dogs (they actually belong to my wife but I love the dogs more than my wife).

* Soccer, triathlons, cooking, movies and staying out of the way of my fiancée and her wedding.

* Volunteer in many sleep-deprivation studies.

* I am an avid bird/sheep/seal avoider.

* Hobbies: Pokemon training and breeding.

* I enjoy cooking Italians and Chinese.

* Drugs and girls.

HOBBIES

* My hobbies include regular attendance at my local gym and swimming poo.

* My home is my biggest interest. I have experience in painting, wallpapering, woodworking, some electrical, some plumbing, pre-finished hardwood flooring, decks and porches, roofing and vinyl siding, just to mention a few.

* I am not a member of any associations, per se, but I do associate well with others.

* My three biggest hobbies are cars, racquetball, golf and reading.

* Throwing parties in clubs.

* Drawing, singing, art, music, surfing the net, collecting Happy Meal toys.

* Some things I like: thin ties. cooking. reading in bed by torchlight. wondering. taking things apart. dogs. making people laugh. sometimes putting things back together. my treasured roman pipe. my bicycle. the

freedom it gives me. black. and white. responsible architects. anything by marcel breuer, getting my hands dirty.

* Charitable work: I temporarily married a man from Romania so he could get his Green Card and begin a new life in the United States.

* Competitive juggling.

* Interacting intelligently with other humanoids.

* Michael Bolton.

* Chess, soccer, cricket bowling.

* I love my diesel truck and gourmet foods.

* Travelling, Golfing, Tennis, Being a Flaming Homosexual, Scuba Diving.

* Raping and famous rapers. Anything by Jay-Z!

HOBBIES

* Speaking in English.

* One time I rode a horse but it bucked me off. I was injured and ended up gaining like 30 pounds, but then I shed that weight like snakeskin.

* Acne lancer.

* General life experience, fibre optics, acting commissioner of fantasy football team.

* Work, putting in overtime, not drinking, smoking or doing anything else that would increase the company's healthcare costs. I do enjoy reading business magazines and upselling.

* Current holder of national record for eating forty-five eggs in under two minutes.

* Although obviously not an 'activity', travelling is one of my passions.

* I have craze of game programming.

HOBBIES

* Planning my wedding – only 298 days to go!

* Surfing the net.

* Maintaining a healthy digestive system.

* Carpentry (like Jesus), smiling politely, carving false idols, fomenting rebellion, feigning concern, reigning supreme, coveting things, laying the foundations for a small cult, drinking my milk before the expiry date.

* I donated my hair to charity.

* Sarcasm.

* My biggest hobby is dishwashing.

* I enjoy doing repetitive things like filing and photocopying.

* Eating, smoking, smoking weed, playing cod.

HOBBIES

* My interests include reading, playing computer games and stamp collecting and I am currently reading Robbie Williams' thought-provoking autobiography.

* Played the lead in Shakespeare's Romeo and Othello.

* Interests: Stalking, shipping, receiving.

* Horse rideing,like going pub when havent got my kids.looking after kids and doing stuff with them when they aint at school.

* Space travel.

* i like playing sport, which i fined gives me a winning appitite for life.

* My interests include cooking dogs and interesting people.

* Painting my toenails in varying colours.

HOBBIES

* Goose enthusiast.

* Sport. I once came close to matching the national record for star jumps.

* Stroking my dog.

* Making others think there's an earthquake by shaking the desks.

* I enjoy all aspects of camping: finding sticks, eating, sleeping, fire.

* Hedgehogs and their lonely world.

* Phishing.

* I love dancing and throwing sex parties.

* I love art, music, theatre and working with people. I am industrious and a very good cook! Also, I love everyone!

HOBBIES

* The sea in all its forms.

* Sitting in the dark watching alligators.

* Memberships: community jazz band, local soccer team, blood group O negative, 'I love the cold side of the pillow' group and 'I would go out of my way to stamp on a crisp fallen leaf' (both Facebook).

* Sport. I played football for Notre Dame before being cut from the team.

* I enjoy reading and movies. Despise jogging but try to anyway.

* Dum major with my high school band.

* Long walks with handsome hubby and bingo.

* Running, sailing, cooking and wondering.

* I sit on my computer for hours.

HOBBIES

* Getting drunk every night down by the water, playing my guitar and smoking pot.

* I love animals and used to own a dog.

* Tournament Scrabble player, amateur stand-up comic and *Jeopardy* hopeful.

* Avid mystery reader.

* Magic and fortune-telling (call for a free reading).

* I love doing all forms of dance, including salsa, ballroom and twerk.

* Playing Trivial Pursuit. I am a repository of worthless knowledge.

* Foraging for mushrooms.

REASON FOR APPLICATION

* To keep my parole officer from putting me back in jail.

* My wife works at your company so I need to be hired as well.

* What I need is a job where I can prove myself. To be perfectly honest, and at the risk of sounding big-headed, when I think of the list of technical requirements on your job ad, the words 'piece of piss' firmly wedge themselves in my brain.

* Not sure, tbh – I think I can probably extend my current temp contract as I have a good commute and I am fairly happy.

* By God's infinite mercy there is always room for optimism.

* The Job Centre wants proof that I am actively seeking employment.

REASON FOR APPLICATION

* What interested me about this job is that it's with a prestigious company (my friends would definitely approve).

* Reasons to hire me: My references have great things to say about me.

* You need me like a general needs soldiers.

* After consideration of my situation from several different angels, I have decided to pursue a new line of work.

* I'll starve without a job, but don't feel you have to give me one.

* I am fascinated by the ever-changing mosaic of mankind and feel I can therefore help your firm.

* I was born to work in newspaper publishing.

REASON FOR APPLICATION

* I think I would be great in the position of book-keeper in a nutshell.

* To be honest I'm not VERY enthusiastic about retail, but I have a fabulous new tie I am dying to show off!

* I am twenty-four years old, which is why I think this position is a great fit for me.

* I definitely possess the drive and dedication to burgeon in this position.

* I'm looking for work because even though my company was profitable last year, this year they are expecting a large defecate.

* I'm not intimated by your internship; I want to be apart of your fun atmosphere.

* I am seeking a new position as I have recently been laid.

REASON FOR APPLICATION

* I will be able to input your agency with a wide and nouveau perspective in the creative field.

* I am anxious to spread my wings in new directions and soar to new heights.

* I was drawn to this global warming research position by my love of penguins and baby polar bears and also I speak fluent Antartican.

* I had a dream last night, and GOD told me that I will get this job, and this is what is right for me.

* I like the perk of company cars.

* Getting this job would look so cool on my CV!

SALARY EXPECTATIONS

* To be paid enough to buy a better house than I and my family currently live in, which has four bedrooms, two and a half bathrooms and a fenced yard. Inflation must be taken into consideration.

* The higher the better.

* Current salary: £36,000. Salary desired: £250,000.

* My compensation should be at least equal to my age.

* I intend to be a millionaire by the time I am thirty.

* Desired wage: Menemum.

* Annual Salary Requirement: −$10.

* The more you pay me, the harder I'll work.

* I'm a class act and do NOT come cheap.

SALARY EXPECTATIONS

* My top motivator is MONEY. If asked to choose between a professional desk job and one sanitizing a barn that pays more, I'm headed for the farm.

* Ideal job would be businessman, with $18,000 to $250,000 in salary, with benefits and the following additional compensation: corner office, receptionist, stocks and bonds, commemorative coins.

* What I'm looking for in a job:
  #1) Money
  #2) Money
  #3) Money

* I need just enough money to have pizza every night.

* My salary requirement is £34 per year.

* I would like to be making £40 an hour. It would help me pay my way through cosmetology school. I want to do hair one day, but first I would work for your company.

SALARY EXPECTATIONS

* My position will have pleasant surroundings, a reasonable salary, low pressure, not require me to bring work home and good benefits.

* Attached is a graph of my salary history.

* I'll need £30K to start, full medical, three weeks' vacation, stock options and ideally a European sedan.

* Seeking any work that is busy and rewarding and employs my vast talents and rewards accordingly. Will take performance-related pay – I am that good.

* Salary, benefits and other requirements: £90,000 per year, plus agreed-upon performance bonus. Four weeks' vacation and ten paid personal days. Company-paid life and health insurance. First-class airline tickets and hotels when travelling on business. Realistic expense account. Office with windows. Secretary.

SALARY EXPECTATIONS

* I need money because I have bills to pay and things to do. I would like to have a life, go out partying, please my young wife with gifts and order entrées consisting of something more exotic than soup.

* Making new start following ruinous bankruptcy. Will require 'golden handshake' upon signing contract.

* I plan to go travelling round the world next year but need to make money to pay for it first, hence my application for this job. So: lots.

* One of the main things for me, as the film *Jerry Maguire* puts it, is: 'SHOW ME THE MONEY!'

REASON FOR LEAVING

* It sucked.

* Having to arrive at a certain hour doesn't make sense to me.

* Frequently on cell phone in front of my boss and also forgot to attend a mandatory meeting.

* I assaulted my former boss. But I have served my time and made a fresh start.

* My boss's son took over the business, cashing out most of it and burning through what was left.

* Being expected to work on Sundays for free is the current problem.

* Any company that insists on rigid time schedules will find me a total nightmare.

* Bounty hunting was outlawed in my state.

REASON FOR LEAVING

* Any interruption in employment is due to being unemployed.

* Charged with inciting religious hatred.

* My boss felt I could do better elsewhere.

* Once again I was made a scapegoat for another person's mistake.

* Was pushed aside so the vice president's girlfriend could steal my job.

* I've been unable to look for work recently due to having ammonia.

* Unfairly dismissed for 'gross incompetence'. Taking former employer to industrial tribunal. Confident of winning.

* Reason for leaving previous employment: I grabbed my boss's boob at the Christmas party!

REASON FOR LEAVING

* I'm not a racist, but sometimes I have a hard time with the unconventional hygiene practices of people from other cultures.

* Left previous job because my boss was stupid and wouldn't listen to me. Left the job before that because my boss was stupid and would always argue with me about how to do my job.

* We stole a pig – but it was only a really small pig!

* I have become completely paranoid, trusting completely no one and absolutely nothing.

* Contract terminated after I was overheard saying, 'It would be a blessing to get fired.'

* My manager dismissed and then blackballed me in the industry.

* My previous employment ended due to lack of work.

REASON FOR LEAVING

* I thought the world was about to end.

* Any break in employment was not intentional.

* Was held at gunpoint and nearly eaten by a giant rodent.

* Left job because disciplinary actions were taken for showing up late.

* It emerged that I had hit my baby's momma over the head with a phone.

* Boring! No money! Hated it!

* They insisted all employees be at their desks by 9 a.m. I couldn't work under those conditions.

* Reason for leaving previous employment: Laid off.

* I met with a string of broken promises and lies. Also cockroaches.

REASON FOR LEAVING

* Unemployed for the past year by choice. Lounging to continue my education when economically feasible.

* My boss kept yelling at me about my punctuality.

* Boatloads of STRESS!

* Husband was boss, left me for waitress.

* Reason for leaving previous employment: Mexico.

* Excessive masturbation.

* Decided not to return after disgracing self at Christmas party.

* I slept with my assistant and it was just really awkward.

* The owner gave new meaning to the word 'paranoia'. I prefer to elaborate privately.

REASON FOR LEAVING

* I was not smart enough to do the job properly.

* Due to irreconcilable differences between myself and the (mis)manager my employment was terminated.

* Current boss is a dick.

* I had a new manager and it was a she and I don't really get along well with females.

* It was hard work.

* Left last four jobs only because the managers were completely unreasonable.

* My current job could literally be done by a partially trained stoat.

* Current commute is a total ball-ache and your office is closer to my flat.

REASON FOR LEAVING

* Everyone hates me.

* They have stopped doing chips in the cafeteria.

* I hold my boss and colleagues in utter contempt.

* Never did I get fired, except once; it was a mutual walk-away. I had a late-night party using the company office building – poor decision on my part, I deserved to lose my job, I learned a good lesson.

* I beat up my boss.

* Made redundant during three months' medical leave following the death of my cat.

* Maturity leave.

* I was fired because I was slow.

REASON FOR LEAVING

* I no longer run my own business due to mismanagement by husband.

* NB: please don't misconstrue my string of jobs as wilful job-hopping. I have never left a company of my own volition.

EDUCATION

* Yale, Harvard and Oxford. Also hold degrees in Business-Running and Profit-Making.

* I finished high school by the skin of my teeth. Spent most of the time daydreaming out the window, but if you hire me things will be different, I swear.

* I have enough knowledge to write an essay on pretty much any subject (without researching it).

* I have a PhD in human feelings.

* I have a uniquely varied education as I attended a number of different schools in my teens.

* I HAVE A BACHELOR'S DEGREE. GIVE JOB.

* MBA, Havrad University.

* During my undergraduate career as a mathematics student, I also found time to win the English department's short story prize, play clarinet at state level, write an article for the school paper about

EDUCATION

the legality of flag-burning (for fun) and learn
enough CSS in a day to build a website for the
nation's foremost transgender attorney. And
much, much more.

* High school was a incredible experience.

* I feel my rigorous education and subsequent
  internship have prepared me for any obstical
  I might encounter.

* Cake decorating I, II and III.

* BA, Small College You Haven't Heard Of,
  May 2011.

* My mediocre grades do not reflect my true abilities
  and standards.

* Education: I went to St James High where my
  parents are both teachers. They are the best parents.
  They met on an airplane to Tahiti in the Seventies
  (my dad travelled a lot for work back then) and he
  thought my mom was just the prettiest stewardess!

EDUCATION

It was love at first sight and they got married four months later. Gramps didn't approve, but he came round after the accident and everything my dad did for him (overleaf), and now it's pretty much an idyllic family life. I attained excellent grades at this school.

* Accomplishment from working in a school system: I survived.

* The focus of my research was on how much worse allergies are when the mould spores that cause allergies enter your body in a frozen state. Not only will you sneeze, but your nose will be incredibly cold, too.

* Graduated in May 2007 with a Master's degree, thicker skin and an overly caffeinated bloodstream.

* Finished eighth in my class of ten.

* Sat final medical exams (failed).

* Attended high school from September 1880 to June 1984.

EDUCATION

* I dropped out of college because I was so oppressed by my **un**intelligent professors.

1977–Present: School of Hard Knocks

Majored in interpersonal communications, with minors in pot smoking and unsuccessfully offering to trade sex with teachers for passing grades.

* I am about to enroll on a Business and Finance degree with the Open University, which I feel will prove detrimental to my future success.

* I posess a moderate educaton but willing to lern more.

* I have a bachelorette degree in computers.

* Graduated: Yes.

* I achieved 28 per cent in my final exam, which sounds bad but the pass mark was 30 per cent, so I was only two points off.

EDUCATION

* I took the same classes and have the same grades as President George W. Bush: no math, no physics, no chemistry, no biology, no common sense!

* I dropped out of law school because I wasn't interested in it.

* Education: Accepted into four out of ten state universities in 1992.

* I have eight years' experience, which I believe equals a PhD.

* If I get my degree, I'll be suitable for anything.

* Bachelor of engineering. Passed out in top 2 per cent.

* Suspected of graduation.

* I graduated in the top 70 per cent of my class.

EDUCATION

* 1994 – Moron University.

* I am studding Business Management.

* Assets: MS in Computer Science. Liabilities: Over-educated. The more I study, the more I become aware of what I don't know.

* High school just bored me.

* I also have a degree English which serves me well in editing text for poor grammer or typos.

* I am currently attended university.

* Man, I fucked up so much in high school. School ain't for me.

* I have a sold academic record.

EDUCATION

* Holder of 98 IQ.

* I have an MA in Communications, a BA (2:1) in English, four A Levels and nine GCSEs. At secondary school I won a prize for creative writing and a silver award for my geography project about volcanoes. Once, we dissected livers in biology and mine was so good the teacher showed it round.

QUALIFICATIONS

* Twin sister has accounting degree.

* None.

* I am Y2K compliant.

* I am properly licensed to operate my vehicle. I have only one offence on my driving record (accidental hit and run).

* I don't run with scissors.

* My father is a computer programmer, so I have twenty-three years' experience with computer programming.

* Have repeated courses repeatedly.

* Master of Marital Arts.

* Professional memberships: Larry's Gym.

QUALIFICATIONS

* You'll be surprised to hear I'm not actually as qualified as you think I am.

* My sister once won a strawberry-eating contest.

* Performed in a local production of *Oklahoma!*

* Technical qualifications: Extremely proficient in Mario Kart for Super Nintendo.

* Sexual assault advocate.

* I can drive, however, I am still in the process of getting my license.

* I have lurnt Word PErfect computor and spreaxsheet progroms.

* Took a special course entitled 'How to Be Patient With an Impatient Boss'.

* Trained in CPR and harassment.

QUALIFICATIONS

* I do not possess any specific HR qualifications per se, but I am a certified lifeguard.

* My qulifications include close attention to detail.

* I am the king of accounts payable reconciliation.

* Watched first season of *The Apprentice* and part of the second season.

REFERENCES

* Ask and ye shall receive.

* You can call my dad or my mum.

* Scott.

* TittyFace Jenkins.

* My landscaper.

* References: REFERENCES UNAVAILABLE BECAUSE THEY WERE ALL BURNED UP IN A FIRE.

* Eric.

* Please only talk to Susan – *definitely* not Claire.

* Who better to tell you about me than . . . me.

* None. I've left a path of destruction behind me.

REFERENCES

* Best not to ask.

* References: DON'T FORGET MAKE UP
  REFERENCE NAMES **

* The Lord Our Father.

* If you get through to Paul, please NB that the thing
  he'll tell you about wasn't my fault.

* Additional references available apond demand.

Please list three references and the time you knew them:	
Sharon Barn	All day long
Nigel Woodm	Wednesday and Friday mornings
Hannah Hamilton	Mainly in the evenings

* I have over 30,000 references available upon request.

REFERENCES

* You could call the people I babysat for last year. I don't remember where they live or what they were called. Their son's name is Jonah.

* Please do not contact my immediate supervisor at the company. My colleagues will give me a better reference.

* That guy that smells like shit down by the subway.

* Please do not call my last boss as a reference. He learned that I was romantically involved with his wife and I was fired to save the marriage. He is unlikely to give me a positive report.

* Neville (dog).

ADDITIONAL INFORMATION

* My family is willing to relocate. Though not to New England (cold), California (earthquakes) or anywhere in the South (people). Chicago would be fine. My daughter favours Orlando's proximity to Disney World.

* Please note: although I'm comfortable checking on patients and administering medication in the form of pills, I am not willing to deal with blood or needles.

* I will be unable to travel for work during the football season when Manchester United are playing home games.

* Have only missed four child support payments.

* I swear quite a lot. Sorry, but I think it's funny.

* For reasons I can explain face to face, if hired, I need to take multiple bathroom breaks each hour.

* Before going into banking I was the bottom half of a unicycle crew that performed at carnivals.

ADDITIONAL INFORMATION

* It's best for employers that I not work with people.

* If you don't hire me, I'll eat a bug.

* I can start immediately because the company I currently work for doesn't want me around any more.

* My frequent job changes over the past few years were the result of horrendous flatulence issues, which have since been remedied.

* Felony for breaking and entering.

* I am afraid of the dark.

* FYI, admin is not my cup of tea.

* This may sound unusual but I work particularly well when naked.

* Available year-round, except for Thanksgiving and Christmas, and August, when I holiday on my father's yacht in the Cayman Islands.

ADDITIONAL INFORMATION

* My availability for work is limited because Friday, Saturday and Sunday are reserved for drinking time.

* Father is a chef.

* Please, before you blow me off as 'overqualified', understand that what I am overqualified for is being a department-store greeter.

* I do have convictions (drug offences), which are from some thirty years ago, when I was 16–18, and I have a caution from four years ago for criminal damage.

* Requirements: You must provide my dogs with mineral water.

* If you hire me, I will return you a big surprise.

* I only drink Pinot Noir (no other comes close) and my preferred snack is smoked salmon.

* I prefer to work alone in maximum privacy.

ADDITIONAL INFORMATION

* Willing to relocate N-E where.

* If I am hired for the position, I hope you will give
  me an office with windows. I'm not very productive
  if I can't see the sun and flowers.

* I own my own tool kit, including an anti-static wrist-
  strap. Home or office call-outs should be less than
  one and a half hours away by public transport or my
  Reliant Rialto.

* I can relocate at the click of your fingers as I
  currently reside in my car.

3.
'WOULD YOU LIKE TO SEE MY YO-YO TRICKS?'

Terrible Tales from the HR Front Line

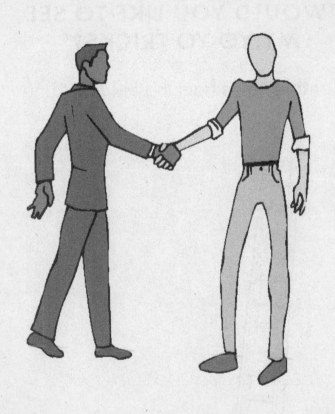

One woman sent her CV and covering letter without deleting someone else's edits in the margins, including such comments as 'I really don't think you want to say this about yourself' and 'This is bullshit, right?'

Q: Do you have any questions for us?
A: Would you like to see my yo-yo tricks?

The CV had a professional headshot of the applicant looking purposeful ghosted in the background.

He had written that he longed to pursue a challenging career within company X – the rival firm of the company to whom he'd sent the application.

The candidate spelled her first name three different ways across her application.

One memorable interviewee called me 'my lady' at the end of pretty much every sentence.

There was a headshot stapled to the CV. Specifically, a headshot of a bulldog wearing a hat, jacket, shirt and tie.

The covering letter was printed on letterhead stationery from the applicant's current employer.

His CV had a number of greasy stains on it and a smudge of what I can only hope was chocolate on the back.

Have you ever been convicted of a felony? Y/N
Yes, arson – will explain in interview.

One candidate sought to prove his reliability by enumerating in great detail the reasons behind the very few sick days he had ever taken – 'housebound by appalling explosive diarrhoea', and so on.

One applicant made a striking impression by using three fonts and eight different colours across her CV, with all the headings given a shadow effect.

One hopeful candidate had printed his application on stationery headed, 'I'd Literally Kill to Work for You!'

One CV arrived in an envelope that had a red car drawn on it. Apparently this would be my gift if I hired him.

The CV was illustrated with a Clipart image of two cartoon people shaking hands.

One candidate turned up to the interview with his mother.

I called the candidate and got through to his voicemail, which was four minutes of gangster rap in which he threatened to do all kinds of dreadful things to 'yo momma'.

Q: In what local areas do you prefer to work?
A: Smoking.

I received a large box in the mail and opened it to find a cast of the candidate's foot with a note attached: 'I just wanted to get my foot in the door.'

When I invited a candidate to interview he asked if we have mandatory drug testing.

One woman applied for a number of jobs with our company over the course of a few years – each time attaching a photo of herself in a season-appropriate costume, e.g. Christmas elf, Easter bunny, giant pumpkin.

This guy turned up for his interview en route to a charity run in which he was taking part. He wore short shorts, had a chicken costume in his bag and jogged on the spot throughout.

I'll never forget the candidate who pulled out a stinking egg sandwich and chomped through it in the interview, explaining she hadn't had time for lunch.

Q: Is there anything about this job that you feel you might not be very good at?
A: Dealing with people.

A woman interviewing for a care position in a psychiatric hospital arrived wearing a turban, a one-shouldered top and sandals that laced all the way up her legs.

When I asked if she felt she was appropriately dressed for the role she replied, 'Don't you think I look pretty?'

An applicant who had not been invited for interview stormed into our building with a case of beer, slammed it down on my desk and drunkenly demanded to know why we hadn't called him back.

I received a picture of the candidate as a young girl working at a hot-dog stand in the summer.

One woman showed up at the interview dressed in a flowered housedress and flip-flops and asked if this was going to take long because her husband was outside waiting in the car.

Q: Choose one word that best summarizes your strongest professional attribute.

A: I am very good at following instructions.

Instead of a covering letter, the candidate sent us a photo of himself reclining in a hammock, on the back of which he had simply written, 'Hi, I'm Sean and I'm looking for a job.'

I once had a candidate include a lengthy anecdote about a family of newts that lived by his garden pond and how he liked to watch them. He had given them all names based on their personalities.

The candidate had spelled 'skills' as 'skelz e'.

One candidate sent us a bag of fried pork rinds with a note saying he'd crunch all our problems away.

The candidate's covering letter was on pale blue paper with hand-drawn teddy bears around the border.

The candidate included a picture of herself in a cheer-leading uniform.

The candidate pulled his phone out and began licking the screen suggestively while maintaining unblinking eye contact with me.

'Um, can I do this on a computer? I usually let Word correct my spelling; it's not a strong point.'

Glitter fell out of the envelope containing her job application, which was written in silver ink on purple paper.

One CV came with a photo attached. The photo was of notorious serial killer Charles Manson. The candidate had used MS Paint to give him bright green eyes and bloody lips.

The applicant's friend came in unannounced, ignored me entirely and asked the applicant, 'How much longer?'

She ate all the candy from my candy bowl in fistfuls
while trying to answer my questions.

One candidate's CV came complete with a debilitating
computer virus that shut down the whole company's IT
system for four days and lost us £2 million in productivity.

When the candidate sat down and crossed his legs,
it became apparent that he wasn't wearing dark
socks with his suit, but had coloured in his ankles
with black marker pen instead.

**Q: How large was the department you worked in with your
last company?**
A: Four floors.

One candidate said that by crossing the Maryland
state line he was in violation of his probation, but
felt the interview was worth risking possible jail time.

The candidate fiddled with her phone and then began
playing the song 'I Feel Good' before finally answering
the question I'd asked half a minute earlier.

One guy insisted on showing us his repertoire of
card tricks during the interview. They were actually
pretty good, if not entirely relevant.

One candidate gave me the distinct impression she
had murdered her husband.

The candidate live-tweeted the interview.

One candidate complained during the interview that she was hot. She then excused herself and removed both socks. After hanging them over the edge of my desk, she continued as if nothing had happened.

The candidate had a horrendous hay fever attack during the interview. At one point she sneezed and a gob of snot shot out and hit me in the eye.

Q: Why do you want to work for this company?
A: I fancy the girl who works on reception.

One woman had created an electronic CV with links to her homepage, where we were greeted with a series of photos of her in the nude.

His CV was printed on the reverse side of a draft letter to another company.

One woman sat with her legs crossed and was nervously swinging her left foot back and forth so vigorously that her shoe flew off and hit me on the leg. She continued as if nothing had happened and ultimately hobbled out of the interview without picking it up.

Admittedly the interview was scheduled for 1 p.m., but I didn't expect the candidate to turn up and unpack their lunch on my desk – picnic basket, cutlery, condiments, toothpicks . . .

> I once had a person clip and file her fingernails while we were speaking.

During an interview in my small book-lined office, the candidate casually leaned back in his chair for a while and then suddenly sat forward again. I didn't have time to warn him that he'd knocked the floor-to-ceiling shelving unit behind him and was about to be buried in books.

> In the middle of our welcome handshake, one nervous applicant accidentally spat his gum out in my face.

On my way to work one morning I was cut up and then sworn at repeatedly by a furious woman in an enormous car. She screeched off ahead of me, making obscene gestures in her rear-view mirror. My burning rage turned to amusement twenty minutes later when she was ushered into my office for her job interview.

Q: How do you handle criticism?
A: I don't let it get me down. I give it right back at the person. I tell it like it is. I'll tell them to fuck right off.

> The candidate kept checking his mobile phone, which was in his hand beneath the desk, apparently under the impression that we hadn't noticed.

At the end of the interview he asked me out on a date.

> One gentleman made a striking sartorial choice when he arrived at his interview with a live yellow snake around his neck. When asked whether he thought it appropriate to bring a snake to an interview, he said that he was trying to set himself apart. We spent the majority of the interview discussing the possible shortcomings of his decision.

The candidate had performed pretty well during a marathon three-hour interview, but then had a sudden panic that he couldn't find his car keys. He had us all search high and low for them and ultimately insisted someone in the company must have pickpocketed him. It turned out they were outside, in the ignition of his unlocked car.

> The candidate had attached a photo of herself dressed as a slutty Minnie Mouse.

This applicant had flown in especially for her interview. Presumably unaware of the exorbitant cost of taxi transportation in London, she had got into a heated debate with the driver over the fare. She refused to pay the full amount when she arrived at our office and the cabbie ended up calling the police while she dashed into the building. In the middle of her interview four officers burst in to issue her with a caution and extract the remaining fare.

I'd applied for a job creating a database for an agricultural company. The interviewer was this rotund, jolly-faced woman who greeted me in a jokey 'farmer's accent', telling me to make myself at home in her office. Feeling at ease I hammed it up and responded, 'Right you are, my loverrr.' This was already less than ideal, but when the interview started I realized with horror that that was actually the way she spoke.

One applicant spent five minutes maligning his previous boss, who I ultimately felt obliged to point out was my father.

Q: Which of these software programs are you most comfortable working with?
A: None of them.

I saw the candidate down a can of Special Brew in the car park before entering our building. It was 9 a.m.

One guy sent his sister to the interview in his place.

The candidate gave me a lengthy bear hug when the interview was over.

When I left work that evening there were posters of the interviewee plastered all over the company parking lot and covering all the windows of my car.

One woman made a memorable impression by showing up in a leather cat suit.

At the time the interview was supposed to start, a barbershop quartet burst into my office instead and sang the candidate's praises.

The candidate arrived for his interview with a cockatoo on his shoulder.

The day after an interview, I received a nice card from the candidate thanking me for my time and asking me to accept the attached small gift as a token of her appreciation. I opened the box to find two cupcakes in the shape of women's breasts.

Our job ad specified that the successful candidate would have to be detail-oriented. One applicant folded his CV into a highly ornate origami Yoda.

Q: What person, living or dead, would you most like to meet?
A: The living one.

A young applicant called Robin thought he'd be cute and send the HR Director a small silver bracelet charm in the shape of a robin. A little morally dubious, yes, but it was nothing compared to what he sent her the following day: a packet of large sponges and a note that read: 'In case my first gift got you too excited . . .'

One guy sent me pictures of his newborn baby.

One woman sent a resume that was formatted like a *Playboy* centrefold, detailing height, weight, vital statistics, likes and dislikes. The photo at least was relatively modest. Under 'biggest turn-ons' she said that she liked intelligent people. She misspelled 'intelligent'.

I received a CV with a teabag stapled to it and a little note: 'Take the time to make yourself a nice cup of tea before you read this. This will be the most important document you read all day.'

Q: How many days, on average, do you arrive late for work?
A: All of the days.

We hadn't advertised a vacancy but one eager jobseeker managed to find the names and home addresses of five members of the board. Having cut out letters from newspaper headlines in the manner of a hate-mailer or hostage-taker, he sent each of them a series of enigmatic notes that gradually spelled out 'Joe Chang is going to blow you away!' The first note just said 'Joe', the second 'Joe Chang', the third 'Joe Chang is', and so on. The penultimate letter proved particularly alarming.

One applicant for a managerial position sent in a five-page CV that listed every single job he had ever done, for money or voluntarily, since he was nine years old.

> I received a clunking great parcel containing a CV that had been painstakingly etched onto a wooden chopping board. I have no idea why.

Once a CV and covering letter floated through my open office window attached to a heart-shaped helium balloon. In his covering letter he admitted he had had 'a little trouble with the law' in his youth, but that the judge had agreed it was a crime of passion and had been quite lenient. It transpired he'd served fifteen years for murder.

> I opened a padded envelope to find nothing but a few hundred candy letters that I was presumably meant to piece together into a message of application.

The covering letter was scrawled in pencil on butcher's paper.

Q: Why do you want to work for our small tech startup, and not, for instance, Google, Yahoo or Microsoft?

A: To be honest, I tried. I couldn't figure out how to apply at Google, Yahoo never called me back and I didn't clear the first interview at Microsoft.

The things she said about her home life strongly implied that her family was in the mob and my life was in danger.

One candidate's resume consisted of literally one sentence: 'Hire me, I'm awesome!'

The covering letter was written entirely in Klingon.

In the field reserved for 'additional materials', one candidate uploaded forty-three photos of himself from birth to adulthood.

Q: It says here that you 'believe in thinking outside the box'. Can you give me an example of your out-of-the-box thinking?

A: Umm . . . Er . . . Well . . . OK, so one time I attended an algorithms class in college and optimized some things for efficiency.

I received an outstanding CV in the post, which didn't mention the candidate's name or any contact details.

I received a four-page CV from someone whose only previous experience was working at a pizza restaurant. She'd listed every stage of the pizza-making process as a separate duty.

I once received a covering letter that discussed, in great detail, a car accident the candidate had been in. Attached was a diagram showing where each

passenger had been sitting, as well as trees and
other notable landmarks along the road.

A mother dragged her teenage son in and filled out
the whole application for him before handing the form
to me. Under 'Skills' she had written: 'I am the oldest
of four kids so I know how to take responsibility.'

There was a link to the candidate's personal blog on
which he had posted a whole series of rants about
wanting to beat up his ex.

I was interviewing a young designer for a graphic
arts job and he'd brought along his portfolio. The first
piece in there was something I myself had designed
three years earlier.

Instead of uploading his CV to our HR portal as
instructed, one candidate accidentally uploaded
his online dating photo: a close-up shot of his (not
inconsiderable) erect penis.

**Q: If you could have a theme song that played every time
you entered a room, what would it be?**
A: That's the stupidest question I've ever been asked.

One applicant had listed the full address of every
company she'd ever worked for, but literally none of
the company names.

I advertised for an experienced camera operator. What I got was a seventeen-year-old kid with zero experience but a three-page list of all the DVD directors' commentaries he'd watched.

One applicant did away with the traditional covering letter and sent us a full-page stock photo of a sunset instead.

A candidate who had evidently been told CVs could be no longer than one page had set the whole thing in size 8 type and reduced the margins to 2 mm. It was basically an A4 sheet of black ink.

Q: What has been your greatest accomplishment?
A: Writing my novel.
Q: Sorry, I meant something you achieved while at work.
A: Yes. I wrote it while at work.

I asked one interviewee to tell me more about the Master's degree he'd listed on his CV. He responded that he didn't actually have a Master's yet, but 'planned on getting round to it someday'.

One applicant sent in an A4 photo of himself standing next to a limousine. No explanation was forthcoming.

A candidate for an engineering position sent in a ream of hand-drawn diagrams of all the technical equipment he had ever used or seen used, with every component labelled using words he'd completely made up.

A woman in her forties sent in a letter that had been scrawled using wax crayons, with every letter in a new colour. At the top of the page there was a vast rainbow containing fourteen stripes.

Half of the CV was an enormous picture of his face. Underneath were his credentials in illegibly small type.

The candidate had looked up every single word in a thesaurus and selected the longest synonym available, whether it made sense or not. Mostly it did not.

I received an application from someone who claimed to have won the bronze medal in Greco-Roman wrestling at the 1992 Olympics. A quick Google revealed he had done nothing of the sort.

Two friends who both worked as builders saved time and energy by sending me both of their CVs in the same email. The CVs were completely identical, except for their names.

Interviewer: That's an unusual surname. You don't know someone called Clarissa, do you?
Candidate: Yes, she's my sister! How do you know her?
Interviewer: She fucked my husband.

There was a photo of the candidate stapled to the CV. She was sitting on a bed in a wetsuit, eating a sandwich.

We received a CV in which the applicant claimed to have worked for us for three and a half years. He'd been telling other employers he worked here and had forgotten to take it off.

At the top of her CV this woman had written a sort of mission statement about how much she wanted a career in beekeeping. All well and good but she was applying for a job as a nurse.

This one man had underlined every single word in his CV and covering letter. Separately.

'I successfully carried out over 3,000 cremations in just four years,' boasted one CV for a job as a school accountant.

Do you have a UK visa? Y/N
No, Mastercard – issued in USA.

I received a 412-page covering letter that was mostly the cut-and-pasted musings of an African tribal elder on the secret healing powers of golden eagles.

Q: Can you identify any areas in which you need to improve?
A: No, none.
Q: None at all?
A: Fine, I guess I'd better come up with something. Clearly
**   *someone* thinks I must have.**

This one guy sent a photo along with his application. He was in a pair of horribly tight Speedos, clutching an enormous cat.

A young woman had got a friend to write out her CV in black marker across her bare back and then sent us a photo of it.

One CV came with a headshot of the late Tupac Shakur ghosted in the background. The CV did not mention Tupac Shakur nor indicate any particular interest in music.

The candidate offered four former bosses as referees, all of whom had fired him.

One candidate sent me a lemon along with his resume, and a note stating, 'I am not a lemon.'

Q: Tell me how you've diffused tense situations with clients in the past.
A: I wrestled them to the ground.

One recent graduate brought her cat to an interview. She put the travel crate on my desk and sporadically stopped talking to play with the cat.

I once had a woman bring a baby wallaby into an interview and let it hop all around our office. Apparently it was too young to be left on its own, her previous wallaby having accidentally broken its neck while she wasn't properly supervising it.

He showed up on a hot July day wearing a single glove in the style of Michael Jackson, dripping sweat through his ill-chosen black clothing. After nervously fiddling with his hair for a while he panicked and made a run for the screen door, which was closed at the time, so it fell out onto the balcony and smashed.

One guy sent his CV and letter along with a close-up snapshot of his penis. It wasn't even a particularly impressive penis.

One man asked me what my star sign was and then accused me of lying, because my answer didn't tally with 'the energy he was sensing'.

A woman came in with her boyfriend to fill out a job application form. While she did so he kissed her neck, nibbled her earlobes and grinded up against her. They pretty much had sex in my office.

I interviewed a man who took his shoes and socks off and rubbed medicated foot powder between his bare toes – in the middle of answering a question.

Q: Are you punctual?
A: Oh yes, I am anally prompt.